Forewor

What Jesus Wouldn't Do

Making the Blind Man Lame

Dr. Michael Johnson

CONTENTS

FOREWORD

Reading this book is like walking unexpectedly into a surprise birthday party. Each new page jumps out with something that catches you off guard. At one moment Michael has you laughing... at the next you are crying. You can see yourself in the honest description of his spiritual journey, and then you are struggling to comprehend the missteps of well meaning missionaries who haven't understood the cultural implications of their actions.

It is likely that some of what you read will make you uncomfortable. You may not share Michael's conclusions regarding the actions and motives of his fellow missionaries, but you will see some of the shortcomings and successes of missions from the eyes of an African American missionary. And you will be the better for it.

You will also see that even though there are unquestionably times when missions and missionaries are flawed, the power of the gospel to change lives cannot be stopped. Today in Kenya, where Michael served for many years, there is a vibrant growing national church, the Africa Gospel Church. This church is a direct result of the investments made by Michael and the many missionaries who came before him and those who have served since him in the lives of their African brothers and sisters in Christ. These African men and women have been eternally changed by the grace of Jesus Christ and through that same grace are now carrying His life transforming gospel to others in their nation and beyond.

The final surprise of this book is captured in its title, Making The Blind Man Lame. When my children were coming of age and I thought they were old enough to understand, I sat them down and shared with them that in spite of my best efforts, my flawed humanity would certainly damage them in some way. Undoubtedly, they would have things to overcome because of the things I did wrong in raising them. Michael helps us to see that in a similar way, flawed missionaries produce flawed disciples, and he challenges us to open our eyes to see this reality and to constantly work to do better.

May God use this book to help us all to do better. As Michael often reminds me, "We are in this together."

Dan Schafer

INTRODUCTION

A CHALLENGE IN BLACK AND WHITE

Keturah, our youngest daughter, was only three years old and a appropriately, a bit naive. We had just arrived in Kenya and were at our first missionary retreat. We were anxious to meet and mix with the other missionaries. It was Keturah's first visit to Africa. What she knew of Africa was the pictures she had seen in National Geographic. She would, on occasion, pick out pictures of partially clad women in tropical climates and proclaim how much they looked like mom. Kay never really took kindly to the comparison.

Keturah was aware there were certain things we should expect in Africa. But she was not ready for retreat with a lot of missionaries. She looked at the crowd of our new co-workers and asked with sweet innocence; "Mom, are we in Africa yet?" (Of course mom should know, she was the one posing in those books.)

Kay answered; "Oh yes Keturah, we have been in Africa for 2 days now."

Keturah responded, "Then why are all of these white people here?"

Thus begins our foray into full time missionary work. We have kind of stumbled around and into asking questions just like Keturah innocently asked. Why are these white people here? What do they really do? What do the Kenyans want from us? Is it necessary that we stay here for long?

It is an easy thing for me to brag about my experience in missions. I have been told by so many that the things I do are magnificent, incredible and worthy of double honor. I have been reminded by many friends and family that since I have given up so much for my faith that I should be rewarded not only in the life to come, but in this life also.

I hear over and over again just how wonderful I am that I have developed a tendency to believe it. To hear some people talk, you might believe that one of the gods is walking amongst them today. I know nothing could be further from the truth, except if you consider the wooden headed idols.

Of course there is nothing wrong with a good healthy self image. But as I allow the Holy Spirit to look deep in the heart of the matter, the truth is that I have too good of a self image. It is precisely this, which scares me. The prophet Jeremiah tells me that my heart is desperately wicked (Jer.17: 9) and I cannot even begin to imagine the evil that is within me. Jesus tells me that out of my heart comes an abundance of wicked desires and dreams (Matt 15:19). No, my problem is not a lack of a good self-image. That is just the problem. I have an image of self that does not jive with that image God has of me.

I already think that I am good enough for heaven. In fact, I felt that I was born good enough for heaven and any slight error within my character could be remedied by a little spiritual deodorant. God was telling me that I needed to be bathed to be clean... bathed in the blood of Christ. It is this revelation that has made me fret when it comes to writing a book about my experience in missions.

I feel as the prophet Isaiah did when he expounded; 'I am a man of unclean lips!' (Isaiah 6:5). However, I have been reminded time and time again by my friend Rev. Elward Ellis that my testimony does not belong to me. Elward was very influential in our decision to do missions full time. Through the conferences he helped put together under the banner of Destiny Inc. God used him to influence us and many other African Americans to open their hearts and minds to service in missions.

God has given me life experiences, which he has compelled me to share with others. This "role model" for missions is less of a foreboding task when looked at the perspective that it is not my story to tell or keep.

This testimony belongs to God and because of this, I must share it in hopes that someone will be influenced to do great things for the Kingdom. It is with this thought in mind, I undertake for the fifth or sixth time, this attempt at writing about Making the Blind Man Lame.

This title is not from an original thought, though I'd like to claim credit for it. I can claim credit for surgical and spiritual misadventures. I didn't invent these either. Suffice it to say, we often do things in surgery and in ministry, which do more harm than good. In our zeal to fix things, remove that mole, take out that lump to make sure it is not cancerous, we can easily do great injury.

We find ourselves flushing the splinter out of our brother's eye with a fire hose and when the brother is on the ground being pushed aside by our torrent of water, we blame him for not holding his eye open wide enough.

Jesus recognized this as a possibility in ministry. This is why when he approached the lame man at the pool, Jesus asked him did he want to be made whole?" (John5:6). Jesus was not presumptuous in healing.

We should be prayerful as the Psalmist is in Psalm 19:13 that God would "keep back thy servant from presumptuous sins, let them not have dominion over me." We need to ask people what they need before ministering to them. This may be un-American, but it is Christ like.

In surgery there are indications and contradictions for doing any procedure. Indications for surgery are things such as, 'severe pain, uncontrolled bleeding or non union in a fracture.' It is easy to overlook these many indications and substitute our own indications; 'we're not very busy, we'd learn something from this and there is good insurance here.'

We can do the same thing in mission's ministry. All sorts of projects get started because 'they look good, we're not busy and we have the money to do it.' We can be guilty of making the blind man lame as we build, start and teach things, which serve to cripple, people who were only blind. We can make people dependent in areas where they were independent.

One of the most important things I learned in my surgical training was how to blame someone for my errors. I was taught to lash out at nurses, medical students and when my superiors were not around, they were fair game also. The game is best played when you can blame the patient. "Oh, if he had only come sooner, or if he weren't so fat, if she weren't so thin. I wish they had told me about those lab results before I started this procedure.' Blame is something I have mastered.

We do the same in our mission work. We blame the patient. The development project doesn't work because, "they weren't ready to take it on, they weren't motivated, and they don't have the insight to plan." We arrive as the specialists for the ailing patient, but quickly blame the patient for his own demise.

Surgeons as a group of people, are not known for being sensitive. I am still learning of my insensitivities as to why a patient gets a wound infection after I have inadequately cleansed his skin for surgery. I would ask him why he didn't bathe before coming to the hospital and make this preparation easier? I forget about the fact that water is unobtainable for many of the people I serve. After 10 years on the field I should not be so stupid as to ask questions like; 'When you urinate, is the water in the bowl dark yellow or light yellow" I am sure many of them wonder; "Why would you urinate in your water (stupid American)" You see water in this setting is too precious to pee in.

As a surgeon, I see things in very stark contrasts. It is either removable or not. The whole world appears to me as 'pre-op or post-op people; that is people who either need an operation or have already had one. There are no in-betweens. I can either do this or I cannot. I have to remember to think of 'Should I either do this or not?'

It is in this light that the spiritual dimension to the ministry gets lost. We all do it in missions. We get so busy doing the work that we forget, as a Catholic priest recently reminded me, that every healing Jesus performed had a spiritual dimension to it. Go and sin no more(John 8:11). Your faith has made you whole (Mark 10:52). All of the miracles performed by Jesus pointed not to himself, but to the Father. It is easy to do good work for the sake of the work and receive the praise unto ourselves and have no spiritual dimension.

I know that it is indeed possible to work for the salvation of the person, the community and the nation. It is indeed possible to help bring salvation to the soul but often at the expense of extinguishing the body, or saving people at all costs..., to them. We do relieve pain and suffering, even when they have arrived to our doorstep with neither.

My friend and missionary surgical colleague Bob Wesche says this about missionaries; 'they are a lot like cow manure. It is a good thing if you spread it around, but heaped together, it can cause quite a stink'. We need to consider our work as finished at some point in time and move on to other projects lest we become a stench.

Maybe we've been here too long. I have my own share of surgical and spiritual missteps in the ministry God has given me. I am writing this book to give some insight for those who would consider how God would use them in other culture ministries. It is also written for those who just like to enjoy a bit of fun laughing at others and themselves. My hope and prayer is that as you read this, you will be sensitive to your own tendencies to 'remove the fly off your friend's forehead with a hatchet,' as the Asian proverb puts it.

I see this as a challenge as clear as black and white. As one of very few black Americans in Christian missions, I know my role to be distinctly different from my white brothers in Christ. As we approach the 21st century, I see black American mission efforts in a light similar to that of the egotistical emperor from Hans Christian Anderson's tale who hired the tailor to make him some fine clothes. Everyone in his fiefdom was afraid to speak against this ruler. However the tailor weaved him a fine suit of clothes made of nothing.

The emperor was so impressed by his own fine figure and certain that no man would dare deceive or delude him, went on to parade his naked frame in public. No one dare tell him he was naked except one bold little boy. This was much to the shame of the emperor, but it did awaken him to his brazen egotistical ways. The black church in America, like the emperor, has no clothes when it comes to mission work overseas. I intend to be that little boy and expose this charade.

We, as black Americans, used to be dressed in fine apparel. However we no longer champion the downtrodden, unless it is our own downtrodden and then only when the white man is the oppressor. We ignore the political and social oppression in Africa unless it is done by those of European origin. We ignore the abuse of human rights in Asia and Latin America because it is not in our supposed homeland. We are only our brother's keeper when we perceive we have akin by skin. This is not the brotherhood Jesus speaks of.

Black Americans frequently ask me; 'How did the missionaries teach the Kenyans to hate one another? How did the missionaries teach the Kenyans to cheat and steal? Why did the Kenyans allow the white man to make them so corrupt? Have homosexuality and bestiality come with the white man?'

To be sure, white missionaries have had some influence for good and bad. However, I would be hard pressed to testify that the origin of these sins are from western shores. Kenyans hated Kenyans before there was a nation of Kenya. Tribes were fighting, killing and hating one another, well before any white face set foot on African shores. Slavery would not have had its successes if it were not for the complicity of Africans against their captive fellow Africans whom they saw as enemies.

White governments took advantage of these situations and exploited old hates and allegiances. This is one way they were able to conquer and control many of the indigenous people by using the strong against the weak. It is these same alliances, which held, sway during colonial days and contributes to the ongoing tribal conflicts these days.

Sexual sin and perversions are present and if you talk with Kenyans they have always been present. It is just not spoken about as freely as it is in America and Europe.

The June 1999 issue of The East and Central African Journal of Surgery documents such cases in Tanzania. The authors suggest that the incidence of sexual abuse in children is not truly known or documented because of the lack of training of professionals to consider the myriad of somatic and psychological complaints children present. In addition, a good percentage of children do not have access to medical care, where sexual abuse cases may be documented and treated. However, they note sexual abuse in children is indeed a real issue in Africa. These things are just not talked about as loudly and openly as they are in the western world. It is not even appropriate for a husband in many tribes to acknowledge his own wife is pregnant. Such information and such talk are forbidden.

We must stop blaming the white man as the only evil. We can leave that to groups of people who do not claim Christ as King.

We pretend that the greatest injustice in our homes today is government sponsored police abuse and are less vocal about the carnage caused by our own children against their cousins and other kinfolk. We have no presence as a force for change in these nations as a part of the body of Christ because we don't make serving the downtrodden and outcast of the world the priority that Christ made it.

We shouted against the crisis in South Africa and we remain silent on the carnage in the Sudan and the casualties of Somalia. In Sudan today, women are having their newborn babies ripped from their breasts, and the babies' bodies smashed against the ground. Missionaries tell me of a mother who was raped by several soldiers, and her breasts are amputated so that she will not be able to feed any of the other children who were sucking. The Lord's Resistance Army in Uganda is well known for its atrocities. Atrocities such as gambling over the gender of the child in a mother's womb, cutting the belly open, slashing through the uterus and removing the fetus to find out who wins the bet. I guess a simple game of checkers doesn't do it for them.

In southern Sudan, villages are pillaged, women are raped as a legitimate means of warfare, while their husbands watch and then are tortured and killed. Those children old enough and strong enough to walk or work, are sold into slavery and forced into Islam as a faith. Another missionary tells of a young boy who is walking along the road with his mother and father. He watches from the bushes, filled with terror as soldiers attack and literally hack his father to death with machetes. Then they gang rape his mother and drag her away to enslave her up north.

If this boy had not hidden in the bush as these horrible things were going on, he himself would have been stolen away to the northern part of Sudan and forced to learn the dictates of Islam. He would be indoctrinated to fight his own people in the south as the soldiers who stole his mother and killed his father.

We as black American Christians are for the most part silent to this tragedy in our midst today. We are waiting for our government to do something, when it is our mandate from Christ. We have no problem pushing the agenda of affirmative action when it comes to our rights. But where is this fervor when it comes to pushing for our responsibilities? How does civil rights match Christian righteousness? Or is affirmative action only an issue when it comes to what we perceive we were denied? If white missionaries were to deny us today the opportunity to serve with them in foreign lands, would we go to court for this right?

Dr. Martin Luther King never intended for the civil rights movement to be a legacy for black Americans. His most fervent calls for justice were for worldwide justice and not for America only. Dr. King used the crisis in America as a beacon to shine the light for freedom and justice in the world. In one speech entitled 'Our God is Able' he concludes with; "...,and God is able to make a way out of no way, and transform dark yesterdays into bright tomorrows. This is our hope of becoming a better people. This is our mandate for seeking to make a better world. Amen!"

The legacy of Dr. King is still exhibited in the work of the Reverend Jesse Jackson who since 1990 has negotiated the release of prisoners of war and civil conflicts from four different nations on three different continents. His recent successful efforts were in war torn Kosovo in May 1999, where he obtained the release of three American soldiers held in that conflict.

This kind of work emphasizes that we are citizens of a world that does not believe black Americans are the only victims of prejudice and hate.

Everywhere I go as a missionary I am asked, "Where are the black American brothers?" My inner spirit response is ; "They are at home, getting ready for the Annual Usher's, Choir and Pastor's Day Banquet. They are frying chicken in celebration of having survived slavery, Jim Crow laws and having won voting rights." We are focusing on celebrating the past and survival. We should be more focused on helping others claim the present and prosper for the future.

My white brothers and sisters will find some saltiness in this series of essays as well. I can't by any means claim to be an authoritative voice. However, there is a great deal of room for improvement on this side of the fence if we truly want to work as one body. The only reason there is a black and white church in America is that white folk wouldn't allow unity. American church history is replete with examples of African Americans being humiliated as they sought to worship with their white brothers in Christ. The African Methodist Church had its origins in Philadelphia due to such rejection as its founder Richard Allen was denied the right to kneel in prayer one Sunday morning.

The black church was forced into this survival mode because there was no alternative. When I was growing up, a 'white Christian' was an oxymoron, because these were the some of the same people we saw defending America in Jesus name, burning the image of the cross He bore. We were forced to survive the Christianity of white folk. Many black Americans still question the sincerity of white missionaries just as we questioned the sincerity of their forefathers who could worship on church on Sunday morning and beat their slaves on Sunday evening.

Just imagine that a white missionary is willing to brave the hot sands of Africa, where tribal war erupts at frequent intervals. Clean water and electricity, are hard to come by. Furthermore, they are willing to travel thousands of miles away from home to do this at a salary that is a pittance to what they would earn in the

US. They will brave diseases of the blood, bowel and brain. They will put their children in boarding schools hundreds or thousands of miles away from where they live and see them at three-month intervals. They will learn new languages, eat new foods learn new customs.

Yet if you were to reassign many, not all of these same white fundamentalists Christians to inner city Chicago or New York, they would most likely say it is too dangerous or too culturally distant. Again I must underscore that there is great sincerity in their call and purpose. And again I dare not make a blanket statement. I personally know of many sincere, earnest white missionary colleagues who have several times risked their lives in African disaster relief, famine relief and war. I dare not and I do not question their call in Christ.

However, many black Americans take notice of this and take it as a double standard. In this light, you can see it is easy to question the sincerity of white missionaries and white mission agencies. This is why the terms "fundamentalist conservative" send chills up the spine of many black American Christians. The terms have, in the past meant to us, segregation, separate but equal, back of the bus and restrictive covenant housing. The term 'conservative' usually means you have something to conserve. We were just trying to survive as black Americans. We had nothing to conserve.

We were forced to survive this duplicity of Christianity that could find the sincere compassion and commitment to the poor of Africa and Asia, while ignoring the same population in America. We know the history of slavery in Africa as many churches participated directly or indirectly in the trade. Those Americans of African descent who do not know Christ look at those of us in the church with awe that we could claim to be of the same body as white Christians.

I myself am always amazed at how my 'conservative-Republican' friends become so 'bleeding heart liberal' when they go to the other side of the Atlantic. I have never seen so much invested in terms of 'understanding, forgiveness and forgetfulness' as I have seen in Africa. With this in mind, I still cringe at the sound of my black brothers who tell me that white Christians only come to Africa to exploit the African. It is hard for me to explain away this apparent duplicity.

However, it would be sheer stupidity of me to ignore the sacrifices and hardships endured by men such as Dr. Ernie Steury and their families of Tenwek Hospital in Kenya. These men and their families went to the hinter most parts of the country without any financial reserves and very little compensation to minister to people who had no one to help them.

I read of prominent people such as former President Jimmy Carter, and Christopher Jordan the founder of Habitat for Humanity, who's families persevered in segregationist Georgia against the odds and showed love and compassion to black people when it was dangerous to do so. I reflect on an interview of former Surgeon General of the United States, C. Everett Koop and how his grandparents who were Quakers were part of the underground-railroad. I am awed at the prospect that they risked their lives and fortunes when it was not politically expedient to do so. However, when most black Americans think about Quakers, we only remember the guy on the oatmeal box and we are not sure if he bought Aunt Jemima to keep her away from Uncle Ben.

I read of how Billy Graham held talks with Martin Luther King and cosponsored revivals with C. Gardner Taylor in Harlem. Rev. Graham even went so far as to hold a banquet in his church in honor of Dr. King, much to the chagrin of his more conservative colleagues in the south. I know there is much to be said about what white Christians have done to undo the misery imposed upon their black sisters and brothers.

Nonetheless, black Americans have survived what many of us see as a double standard of Christianity. In much of America well into the mid 20th century, black men and women were denied the right to congregate even for funerals unless a white man was present.

We were denied the right to dress in shirt and suit and tie except as preachers or deacons. Hence the need to dress to impress exists today in black America. We are still 'faking it without making it.' We wore our survivorship proudly because it was what we were allowed to wear.

We now wear our tailored suits because the white power structure would not allow us to wear any other garments. We were not allowed garments such as self-respect, self-reliance or self-determination. The fine tailored suits are our evidence of having survived and succeeded in a nation determined to make us fail. These expensive garments we now wear in excess as we believe our access to excess is success. We have missed the point.

It is only within the last decade of the 20th century, over 130 years after the civil war, that the Southern Baptists have admitted that slavery was evil and asked forgiveness of black America . Even with this admission, the vote was not unanimous.

There are multiple reasons for our absence from the mission fields and they find their root cause in our own perception of self. White people have been white a long time. Black people have been evolving since the nation's beginning. From the nation's inception we were not considered people. To be more specific, we were legislated to be only 3/5 human for the sake of political peace in these United States. Article 1 of the United States Constitution assured our non-human status for centuries.

Hence as white people have been white people a long time, we have evolved from being a portion of a human, a thing, a colored person, nigger, nigra African, colored, Negro, black, African American and in many instances from ourselves, nigger again.

We are a bit schizophrenic. W.E.B. Dubois says it is a miracle that we are able to survive as a person as we have always been a 'problem' for America. "....How does it feel to be a problem? ...one ever feels his two-ness, -an American, a Negro; two souls, two thoughts; two unreconciled Strivings; two warring ideals in one dark body, whose dogged strength alone keeps it from being torn asunder."

We black people still wrestle with the persistent perception within American culture that we are an ignorant, uncivilized people, unfit for service to God or man. Tarzan was required to come and teach us manners in the jungle and now the State Police have taken up this role. We constitute less than 13 percent of the population but are villanized as >80 percent of the criminals. How can we subdue the earth for Jesus when we are so unfit?

Black Americans still function in a white world where we have never been allowed to realize we are part of its maintenance or its prosperity. If we cannot function well here, what makes us think we can function well overseas?

White people are not used to having black people or any non-whites tell them they are in error. My white brothers and sisters must recognize that they can make mistakes. Because they have been the dominant voice in world missions for so long, it will be hard for them to hear this from a novice in the field. Most Americans believe that white Americans actually introduced Christianity to Africa. I am sure that many white American missionaries are under the same misconception. However, to believe this is to completely ignore the Biblical record of Africa.

Isaiah in the eighth century B.C. lists several portions of Lower Egypt and Kush. The Ethiopian eunuch whom Philip met on the road to Gaza from Jerusalem is part of the Biblical record. The name Simeon 'the black' and the teacher Lucius from Cyrene are just a few other names in the Biblical record. Egyptian Christianity flourished in the first century as part of the Coptic tradition, and we have recently been made aware of the Jews of Yemen who were reunited with the political state of Israel in 1948 and 1962.

In other words, the Judeo-Christian traditions are not new to Africa. In point of fact, this faith is being reintroduced and catching like wildfire. Elizabeth Isichei in her book, The History of Christianity in Africa notes that 'while 7,500 people denounce Christianity in the west everyday, twice that number claim Christ in Africa every day.' However, white Americans have written most of the accepted history of the United States, and rarely are they perceived as the 'bad-guy'. This type of historical interpretation tells you that you have all knowledge and all power, it is difficult to think or admit that you could be wrong.

Now these statements may sound racist, but because 99.99999 percent of the American missionaries were white, these are still true statements. Please, don't get too defensive on me now.

When I walk into a room and I see a broken glass and there is only one of my children in the room, I never need to ask; "Who broke it?" I ask anyway and they generally are inclined to tell me; "I don't know. It was broken when I came in." It doesn't take a whole lot of detective work, usually.

White people were for the most part the only ones doing the hard and necessary work of planting missions. By default, they also bear the blame for the mishaps. This is not meant to offend, it is just a matter of fact. It is estimated that of the 45,000 missionaries from North America, only 250 are black Americans.

Again, remember black people aren't just paranoid without reason. Just remember the last time a group of white people invited a group of some 20 million or so black people on an all expense paid voyage with non-reserved seats across the ocean. It was first come..., first to serve. It was not a good experience. We are also well aware of the fact that no native American, or Indian as they are called, will ever sign a land development deal with a white man without some reservations (for lack of a better word). History has shown some interesting precedents.

So if it seems as though I am generalizing here, I am just stating what the statistics bear out. Black people have not been there to do some of these things. If we had been there like we were supposed to be, we would have undoubtedly made many of the same mistakes. Since I have arrived in missions, I have proven this to be true. I have made many of the same utterances, held many of the same biases and prejudices. I have my own set of tribal slurs, which one could easily substitute for racist slander. So please, my white brother, don't get too defensive. We are all fallen flesh.

It was white missionaries who taught that church buildings are important and hence, we have built some very large church buildings in Kenya. In many of the regions in which we have built these church buildings, people are starving or at least very malnourished. I know that many of those families who were starving contributed to the building of these churches. They sold their farm goods and sacrificed many of the comforts and provisions for their families in order to build some of these churches.

Many of these people who attend these churches do not have Bibles. Many of these people could not read a Bible even if they had them. These church buildings can cost tens of thousands of dollars. I don't understand how we became a part of making the blind man lame. I don't know how we can build church buildings, which cost multiple thousands of dollars in the middle of illiterate, malnourished people.

I feel there must be some better way to invest our money other than to have a man explain to his wife and children that the God they serve is happy that he has sacrificed his sparse crop in order to build a church building. I don't think this really encourages the young families to follow our God.

I would hope we could encourage people to have church house meetings with Bible study done by the fireside in mud and stick huts occupied seven days per week, instead of not reading Bibles in brick and mortar buildings which lie vacant most of the week.

One extreme example of this is found in the massive Catholic cathedral in the village of Yamoussoukro, Ivory Coast, which was build at a cost of over 200 million dollars. This cathedral, Our Lady of Peace, is the largest Christian church edifice in the world. Like St. Peter's, which the Protestants of 16th century Europe scorned as a scandalous extravagance, Our Lady of Peace is being maligned as an unseemly expense in a country with an annual per capita income of $650. Demands a devout Ivory Coaster: "Why build a church for God while there are so many unemployed and near starving?" (Time; 1989; pg 38:July 3).

Missionaries have built schools, hospitals and a variety of industries at no expense to the church or the communities in which they serve. To the credit of the missionaries with whom I work, there is a lot of development work being done in the regions of Kenya.

Missionaries have used the Bible to speak on essential things such as holiness, and tithing to the exclusion of the issues of self-respect and pride in Christ. Kenyans today still wrestle with racial inferiority, which they feel acutely when they meet white missionaries. This inferiority persists because the examples of Christ they see are successful white men and women who have computers, nice cars, nice homes and nice clothes.

The Economist magazine of May 2000 had a printed a series of articles which underscored this, stating that Africans had lost their sense of pride as a direct result of colonialism. As I sit and talk to and read about the history of whites in Kenya, I am impressed that this feeling of racial inferiority plays an immeasurable part in what we see in Africa today.

I have seen several examples where missionaries are not only building the church, but also building the people.

Kenyans see pictures of a white Jesus, a white Moses and even a white Simon of Cyrene in the much-touted 'Jesus' film. There is little if any depiction of anyone of color in the Bible in a positive role. I heard one black comedian say that if white folks made a movie of the history of slavery in the US, they would have an all white cast. This may be a bit extreme, but the point is, we as a people of African descent on both sides of the Atlantic are of the opinion that we must model ourselves after the dominant culture in order to succeed.

To be a good Christian in many Kenyans eyes is to model their lives not after the Christ they learn of in the Bible, but after the missionary they see. This is good and bad. However, Jesus never associated doing the Father's will with the entrapments of western culture. As I look around in Kenya I see celebrations of Christmas with trees and ornaments and even Santa Claus. If it comes from the west it will be mimicked and it assumed to be Christian.

To be a good Christian is to take on all the things the whites have to offer because obviously, they come from a better culture. If the Kenyans will follow them as they follow Christ, material impoverishment will cease and they can have a microwave too. Elizabeth Isichei in her "History of Christianity in Africa" expounds on the cultural imperialism that many of the Africans felt was imposed on them by the missionaries. It was not Christ that the Africans were embracing, but western culture and religion. This does not build the people to be who God is calling them to be, but rather who we expect they should be. We make them in our own image.

We need to address the issues of self-respect in Christ, self-reliance in Christ and self-determination in Christ if we want to be effective in the roles we have been called to fill. For white missionaries who come from a culture, which tells them they are superior because of their skin color, this is impossible without a special work of grace by the Holy Spirit. However, these are things God would have us impart. There are many Kenyans who feel they were born to pick the white man's tea. I have been told so by many who came from tea farms.

The educational, commercial and industrial infrastructure of Kenya does not allow the average Kenyan to achieve the successes the average missionary has achieved. Most new conversions to Christ in Kenya are made by other Kenyans. However in a mission compound setting, a new Kenyan convert to Christ starts to measure his or her lifestyle comparing it to the western missionary. The comparison makes it obvious that something is wrong in the Kenyan's walk with Christ. He doesn't have the material blessings, so either he has read the Bible wrong, or God is not keeping track of how well he is performing. Since God cannot make mistakes, there must be something wrong with his Christian walk.

This must mean he or she needs more education in western schools, sponsored by people from the west. Therefore, there is a need to dress to impress the donors and to take on their lifestyle, worldview and values. In order to support these new habits, more money is required. Hence we take a young Kenyan Christian convert and make him after our likeness, in our image.

It is difficult for this young convert to minister to 'his own' people and encourage them of their unique worth in the Savior's eyes. Because then he must leave all that he is behind and model his life after other people in order to better care for his own kind. How does he impart self-respect, self-reliance and self-determination for his family, his community, his church and nation with this scenario?

How does he after having done much learning, return to a lifestyle in a small village that has no water, no power and no significant commercial enterprise? It is much easier for this learned scholar to stay in the city. It is even easier for him to stay overseas. We make a blind man lame. Just ask the average missionary who has been on the field for more than 10 years if this typical convert is more or less dependent upon the west.

I believe we are continuing to make the blind man lame. We can break the cycle, but it will require us to consider ourselves as part of the problem. For the black American we must admit we must become part of the solution. For the white American, let black America give you a bit of insight God has given us in 500 years of associating ourselves with you. We can learn from each other and Christ will be glorified in the body in the process. People will marvel at our joint efforts and say; "Oh how those Christians love one another!" Our Lord made this observation; "By this shall all men know that you are my disciples if ye have love for one another." (John 13:35)

PERSONAL AND FAMILY COSTS OF DOING MISSIONS

I DIDN'T WANT TO BE THAT GOOD.

The American author and radio personality Garrison Keilor was heard to relate the story of holding his newborn baby daughter in his hands. He tells of the joy of holding new life. It was such a joy to behold a soft and innocent baby in his arms. He knew his daughter would forever change his life. She would require constant attention. She would require sacrifice. She would require him to change. She would require him to be a better person. He would have to be good. Then he went on to admit, "I didn't want to be that good!"

I guess when it comes down to it, I really don't want to get too close to Jesus. I don't want to be that good. We all wrestle with this somewhat. The more the Holy Spirit becomes real to me, the more I am inclined to have second thoughts about this burden for missions.

You see, I became a Christian reluctantly. I was really enjoying all of the things in which I found myself involved. I enjoyed smoking dope (oh yes, I did inhale). I enjoyed having any woman who would be willing to spend a little time with me.

I enjoyed the attention of being among the elite intellectuals within my small congregation of a black Baptist church. I enjoyed buying new expensive suits and shoes on a whim.

I enjoyed a life without real sacrifice. I enjoyed giving what was left over out of the abundance God had given me. I enjoyed going out to dinner for any occasion, spending whatever it would take to keep my wife happy and impress my friends. I enjoyed buying those four new cars in five years.

I enjoyed having a beeper, a phone in the car and the ability to hire two staff members in the office to manage my growing patient load. I enjoyed the new computers we had purchased for the office and being able to dictate letters to the referring physicians detailing how I removed the skin tag from one man and the gall bladder from his wife.

Why did I need to do overseas missions? I really don't want to be that good. That is the problem with Christianity. The more I read the Bible, I find that there has to be something to the admonition Christ lays out about 'seeking the kingdom first' and having the needs of life met in the process (Matthew 6:33). I don't want to be that good however, because it will cause me to live out this goodness. It will cause me to 'sell all I have and give to the poor and follow Him.(Matthew 19:21).'

I don't want to be that good because it will not allow me to store up treasures in this life, but cause me to think more about the life to come. Who needs that?!? I really want to enjoy life here Lord. I told Jesus this on several occasions. This idea of bringing every thought captive to Christ (2 Cor 10:5), means that I can't even think bad thoughts, watch bad movies, tell bad jokes or keep bad company, at least not for pleasure.

What good is this sterile life? How can I be of any use to God if I don't enjoy life. I don't want to be so good that I have to be that weird thing called 'holy'. Holiness and godliness are attributes for losers who wear out of date clothes, drive old cars and watch dull movies in black and white. I don't want to be that good. Just let me be good enough to appear to be good.

Just let me wear the cross around my neck without carrying the burden in my heart. "I promise I won't stray too far from you Jesus!"

Well as we all know, God never does things halfway. I came to know the Lord as my Savior as a young boy. I didn't truly allow Him to be Lord of my life until I was in my junior year of college. There, after having done all of the wrong things, I knelt down and opened the Bible my mother had given me my freshmen year. I asked the Lord to prove He was truly who He claimed to be by coming into my heart and doing what He said he could do.

Weeks later, I was on a date. I had one thing in mind for this young lady. I would amuse her. I would overwhelm her with my charm. I would then do what everyone else was doing in those days of 'do your own thing'. As I laid out my plan on the date, I found something kept bothering me. I would want to say little fleshly nothings in her ear and it came out as spirit filled somethings. Someone was interfering in my game plan. If I had known this was going to happen, I would never have invited Him into my heart!

The young lady looked at me in amazement. She asked; "What are you some kind of fanatic or something!" Well, needless to say, the night was only downhill from there. I did not get what I wanted, because God answered my prayer. He did what He said He would do and started 'giving me the desires of my heart' which He promised in Psalm 37:4. As I understand this verse it means God would actually change the desires of my heart. He would actually make my heart desire other things than it would normally. In that sense He would give my heart the things it should desire.

When I was in medical school at the University of Michigan, I attended New Hope Baptist Church. Dr. A.J. Lightfoot was my pastor there. He was my mentor and friend. I admire him greatly for the tremendous influence he had upon me. One day he was preaching and he threw the Bible on the floor and put one foot on it. Then he proclaimed "You must be able to stand on the word of God!" It was the most vivid illustration I have ever had of how much I must learn to depend on God. I didn't have to make myself good. God could do it if I would yield to His word.

I still struggle with being good. God has built a hedge around me. I have my wife to remind me of my tendency to err and of course my kids constantly keep me in check as I must be what I want them to be. I do believe that 'He is increasing as I am decreasing' as John states in John 3:30.

ARE THERE MANY MZUNGUS IN PUTU LAND?

There were cows where the plane was landing! How is this pilot going to put this plane down in the middle of this field when the cows are grazing? As I look closer, there are also people down there. Lots of men could be seen, working with sickles or slashers, cutting the grass for us to see the rocks and holes on our landing strip. If I had known the trip to Zaire in 1984 was going to be this kind of adventure, I would definitely have second thoughts.

I look over to see my wife. We've only been married seven years. What will people say about us now?

Have you heard about Michael and Kay? They left their kids in Philadelphia and flew to Africa somewhere out there! The last anyone had heard from them was they were in some small plane and it went down in the trees. The lions, tigers and bears have probably devoured them by now. Oh my! What will the children do now?"

My mind comes back to the pilot now as he eases the throttle back in and radios to someone down below; "Hello Tandala Hospital, this is Papa Zulu, this is Papa Zulu. Do you read me? Over."

The message shoots back, "Roger Papa Zulu, this is Tandala. We read you and you are clear to land" Now it hits me. "That ain't no control tower! This guy is talking to someone in a thatched roof house, with a radio antenna on top of it! Is this some kind of joke? So what if they think it is okay to land. What comfort is this? Did anyone ask the cows if it was okay to land? Or are we just being polite?"

The pilot buzzes the field twice and the workers stop slashing the grass and chase the cows off the field. We circle the field once more and begin our descent to land.

I look over at Kay as if to say; "Isn't this fun sweetheart!"

She looks back at me, her eyes saying; "Wait until my lawyer hears about this!"

She did have some legitimate divorce claim if she sought to file it when we returned. We had never discussed missions in our whole married life. When we planned this trip, it was supposed to be a vacation. I had just completed my surgery residency and we both felt a time away from Philadelphia, alone, in the tropics would be good. She chose the Bahamas. I chose Zaire. She was the better Christian in letting go of her own desires to fulfill my felt call.

'Well after all, it is warm, has palm trees' I thought, 'maybe she won't notice.'

Of course, that is not what she is thinking about now. She just wants out of this small van with wings. Both of our stomachs are churning as this plane bobs and weaves with each passing breeze.

'Hmmmm. One engine! That's interesting. What happens if...?'
Perish the thought.

I am reminded of the dangers of such a flight as we consider
the World Gospel Mission missionaries lost over the jungles of
South America in the fall of 1998. The pilot, his family and passengers were all lost and despite the efforts of the US Government
Armed Forces sponsored search of the jungles, they remain 'missing in action', even in the summer of 1999. If I had known the
trip entailed such a flight, I would never have volunteered.

The plane lands. We get out and are immediately surrounded
by dozens of smiling, excited Zairians. They laugh and reach out
to touch us and help us with our bags and belongings. They are
excited because of the plane of course, but also, it is the first time
any 'black-white' people have come this way. Well the real term
for this is people from putu land (pronounced POOTOO).

Putu land is anywhere that is not within walking distance of
their familiar surroundings. Putu land is where all of those planes
come from and hence all of the people on the planes are PUTU
people.

We found it funny being Putu. We had no idea of the fact
that these people could have such a limited worldview. How
could they not know we were not just coming from some single
place called Putu? How could they not know we were from different cities and different nations than some of these missionaries?
Hadn't any of them seen a map or read a book?

One day during our stay in Zaire we met some people who
had some idea of Putu history. They were amazed that Kay and I
had come to visit them.

They were sad about the fact that we had to overcome such
odds to do so. When Kay and I asked them what obstacles they
spoke of they related that we had to escape our slave captors in
order to visit them in Zaire today.

They were amazed that a man of my color could find a wife of my own color way over there in Putu land. Are there many people like you over there? It was obvious they needed an update on Putu history as many people went on to express their sorrow about our continuing enslavement in America.

When I chuckle at this, I think on some of my own friends and family who have no broader view of the world than their big screen television. They actually believe they can travel the world by switching the channels of their cable television.

They don't want to complicate that travel by watching The History or Learning Channel or listening to Public Radio. They would rather focus on the good stuff, the sit-coms and soap operas.

When we talk with them about travel to Africa the kind of questions we get are; 'Don't they have drive in banking? Or, can you bring me some gold and diamonds when you come back? and Have you ever been attacked by a lion?" I am amazed that we have the Putu mentality here in the US.

I know the Kenyans laugh at us. That is why the call us Mzungus. The Swahili word comes from Kuzunguka, which means to go around. An Mzungu (pronounced mm-zoon-goo) is any person who spends a lot of his or her time, running around. That pretty much describes what we do and how we appear to the average Kenyan. So I know that every time I am called an Mzungu the Kenyans are laughing at us inwardly. I do know that many Kenyans really think that all white people look alike!

Kenyans do laugh at us. I have the privilege of African camouflage and I have heard them ridicule us as though my camouflage did not matter. It is widely held that when missionaries arrived they had the Bible and the African had the land. After a moment of prayer with eyes closed, the African had the Bible and the missionaries had the land.

I have heard this story from Kenyans. Many believe that they were given colored beads in exchange for their precious stones and gems.

I found it funniest when the Kenyans themselves tried to translate Mzungu to mean just white people. Originally the only non-black people Kenyans would encounter were white people or Indians (from India, not those from West Virginia). Now, however, many people of many nationalities and colors come to Kenya and it confuses the average Kenyan in the 'up-country' villages. Thus, I have been called the 'white man' in many local Kenyan churches.

Some of our black guests from Philadelphia have taken a lot of offense at this. "We've been through enough teaching in 'black pride' so we don't have to be insulted by being called white!"

Kay cautioned our black American friends to not take offense at being called white people. It was not a depiction of their color, but of their lifestyle. 'You are a white person, you are Putu because you obviously have clothes to change everyday and you carry cameras and get into and out of cars and come and go constantly. You are a white person not because of how you appear by color, but by your lifestyle.'

The challenge to us as we approached missions work overseas was to take the blinders off. We needed God to help us deal with our fears and suspicions. We needed God to help us see the rest of the world and not be concerned with our small corner of it. He sent His son to die for all of the world, both Putu and non-Putu, for the white man and the black white man, for all Mzungus wherever they are. Besides the Bahamas would have been a boring trip compared to Zaire and the adventures, which awaited us in the years ahead.

JESUS MADE ME LOSE MY MIND.

I don't want to appear to avoid him, but he sure looks strange. As I try to hide behind the group of people talking about how much they miss shoveling snow and all of the fun things of winter, he starts to approach me. Oh no, I'm gonna have to meet this guy. What kind of way is this to spend Christmas?!?

It was a Christmas afternoon in Africa. This is not about the nativity scene. It is about a Christmas afternoon in Africa in 1987. Nairobi Kenya is where it happened to be exact. Not only am I trying to avoid this mystery guest, I am also gonna get stuck watching a movie I dread, White Christmas. I have learned over the years, however, that in order to keep peace in the home, I must be a husband that sits through a lot of chick flicks. Am I being insensitive here?

We were invited to share Christmas dinner with this missionary couple and the feature film was Bing Crosby and Danny Kaye in White Christmas. It is bad enough that there is no football with the wonderful TV commercials. It is bad enough that there are no phone calls from grandmom and no sweet potato pie. We are pretending it is Christmas and there is no hint of snow on this 85 degree day and spraying white stuff on the windows which the Kenyan house helper will have to scrape off somehow. (Crazy Mzungus!)

Everything is just right. Our host and hostess couple is gleeful. The Christmas carols are playing. The invited guests are arriving right on time and everyone seems happy and at home. Everyone except for this one guy. This black guy. He seems somehow out of place. He is a guest in the home, so who am I to question the guest list?

He's coming towards me now. He looks odd. He is about 6 feet tall. He looks like he has been on some kind of radical diet plan. As he comes closer, our host arrives to introduce us. "Michael this is Jerry." I hold out my hand and force a smile. Jerry does likewise and reveals swollen gums and loose teeth. I think; 'I don't remember Nutri-System promising this.' His cheeks are drawn and his eyes have that shallow sunken look which says, 'Why me?'

Our host goes on to tell me about Jerry. Jerry is a black American surgeon. He has been working in Kenya for about one year. Well actually less than one year. Three months of his time he has been a guest of the government in one of its jails. It appears that Jerry upset someone of influence in the halls of government and they provided him with accommodations rent free for this offence. International human rights organizations frequently deplore the conditions within Kenyan prisons.

Jerry had lost 30 or 40 pounds. He had gotten scurvy. This explains his lost teeth and thinning hair. As he describes his experience he tells of a room with a hole in the middle of the floor where he and the other 6 or 8 men could relieve themselves when necessary. There were no blankets provided so one had to get by on what one wore into these accommodations. Food was given daily, slid through a space between the bars of this cell and shared with the other inmates. If you missed your chance, you had best hope there was family or friends on the outside to bring you food. It was good to be aggressive in this situation if you wanted to eat.

Jerry had only raggedy clothes. His passport was stolen. Our host and hostess had gotten him out on a Christmas release. They wanted to know if I could help him out. I wanted to know if they were pulling some kind of bad stunt.

What were the odds of meeting another black American surgeon in Kenya. There were probably fewer than 1,000 in the world. There were probably...., 2 celebrating Christmas in Nairobi.

Now I ask the Lord, "Have you lost your mind? I am feeling you call me into missions and this is how you want to introduce me to the call?"

Then Jesus reminds me that indeed he did lose his mind. He hid his will within his Father's will. Jesus always did the things which pleased his Father (John 8:29).

He then reminded me that was exactly what he wanted me to do. Philippians 2:5 tells me that I must let His mind be in me..., humbling myself to His will as he did for the Father.

I believe God was asking me if I was willing to go anywhere in spite of the obstacles. Could I see the danger of being obedient and still stay steadfast? Could I see myself in this man, knowing how much this had cost him and still seek to be obedient? Was I willing, like Jesus to lose my mind?

JUST BLAME YOUR WIFE.

First of all, I didn't invent this one, though I tried it out. I had gone to the Lord about this call in missions. I didn't want to go. I still struggle with this call, even as we get ready to return to Kenya for our fourth time. We are ten years into this mission now and I still wonder how I got into this. I almost got out of it at one point. I was going to blame my wife. I figured, 'Hey, Adam tried it..., why not me?'

Of course I denied the fact that Adam's plan didn't work, but maybe he just didn't pursue it enough. You see, I read the book. I had better lines than Adam to defend myself from God. Lines like "Am I my brother's keeper?" and, "Who is my neighbor Lord?" I could convince God that I would go to Africa if my wife wasn't so caught up on creature comforts.

So I gave God this as a reason. I had just bought my wife a diamond ring to celebrate our tenth wedding anniversary. I had bought her a car for her birthday and a fur collar coat for Christmas. We had renovated, painted, landscaped and upgraded our home in suburban Philadelphia in so many ways that we didn't recognize it ourselves. The kitchen had every electronic gadget known to man, Martian and moon man. We were looking at more real estate at a better house in Cherry Hill, New Jersey, a nice home with a nice swimming pool.

I knew my wife wanted more than what I could give her in missions. We had spent some time in Zaire where we saw missionaries living with and being bitten by every kind of bug on God's green earth. I once counted and Kay had at least one hundred mosquito bites. She can't stand bugs and we both hate bats, even though we later went hunting for bats at night. We had slept in houses with bats flying overhead at night.

We had traveled by truck on roads more suited for ox carts and flown in planes which were the size of an easy chair with wings. My wife would vomit on these flights. She hates these small planes. Who looks for you when you go down in the midst of all of those trees in the rain forest?

So I went to a good friend of mine for advice. How could I get God to see that I was a willing servant, but my wife was holding me back? My friend reminded me of my wife's desire for a new Jaguar car, in a dark kinda army green color. "How can you buy her Jaguar, he asked me, if you go into missions?"

I had every reason to blame my wife for not going. Kay had never lived outside of Ann Arbor Michigan until we married. Moving to Philadelphia for my surgery residency had proven very traumatic for her. I knew there was no chance of her moving to Timbuktu or outer Mongolia! After all, she liked to watch Oprah on television, getting her nails done and hair do (or is that 'hair did') frequently.

She had already seen the malls of the Zaire jungle and the novel thing they sold was, not live lobster crawling in saltwater tanks, but dead monkey hanging on hooks. She had already gone to the butchery in Zaire, which was one of the missionary's home where we helped dismember and disembowel a freshly killed cow. The disemboweling had to be done quickly before the ripening of its contents, or the exercise of butchering was no longer fun.

Speaking of cows, what are those funny things that the milk comes out of? Then, when the milk comes out, its warm and it has hair in it! The 'milk lady' comes to the door to sell it to you and you have to strain it, filter it and boil it before you can cook with it or drink it. No, no, my wife would not stand for this kind of back to nature living.

Even when we would go camping with our $300 Coleman tent with lanterns, sleeping bags, inflatable mattresses stove and bottled water in upstate Pennsylvania, she would somehow manage to take at least four pairs of shoes one of which had high heels. What would she do with all of those hair curling irons and how could she plug in her rollers on a mission compound with only a few hours of electricity from a diesel generator?

I was sure I could depend on my wife to say "No way Jose! I ain't gonna live in a place where getting a run in your best stockings means escaping a warthog's tusks while wearing your finest pantyhose." So I had God on the ropes now. I was willing and it was His turn to make His move. I had outwitted the Almighty. So I signed on, testing God.

We went to our mission headquarters at WGM in the spring of 1988. We listened to the folks there. We met with the various vice presidents and officials of the variety of offices. We finally got down to meet with the people in accounting. They were the ones to calculate our salary. Well, that is what they call it, a salary. When it was presented to me, it sounded more like an allowance you would give to your kid in college. Now I knew this would be the final blow.

As the man sat there with a very serious face, he wrote down what it would take to support me and my family of six on a monthly basis. He never cracked a smile. He was dead serious (as serious as a heart attack we might say). He gave us a figure for our monthly salary.

I started sweating, my mouth got dry and my head started spinning. I wanted to be let out of this room quickly. I needed some air! I felt queasy and ready to scream. I looked at him like as if to say; "Surely mister white man, you can't be serious!"

I looked at Kay expecting her to be in tears. She looked as placid as someone who had just had a frontal lobotomy, electro-shock therapy and a heavy dose of Prozac all in one setting.

I looked back at the accountant and said "No, I mean how much do we make per month?" Kay kicked me under the table. The surgery, electricity and drugs obviously did not have the desired effect. I wanted to kick her back.

I wasn't joking when I asked this question. It was obvious this man didn't know how to add up what it would take to support this woman and her children! I was making more per day than he was telling me I would make per month. What was the meaning of this? Were these people serious? Maybe there was something in the Indiana water.

Maybe my wife was part of some plot to undermine the very foundation of our family. Maybe they had gotten to her and were trying to get to me. My mind was spinning. My last hold out was not holding out.

She had seen the paltry income and it did not hit her that this would not allow her to stock the freezer, refrigerator, closet, pantry, storeroom, garage and basement with everything on sale.

She had been to Africa and somehow she forgot that the only thing discounted there was old soft brown bananas and older hard white corn. We had been on the muddy streets of the market where half carcasses of fly covered beef hung in windows baking in the hot sun next to the entrails of goats smoking on charcoal grills. And speaking of keeping your meat cool, she had seen the kerosene-powered refrigerators which did okay as long as kerosene was available. This was not like buying Colorado Prime for your freezer.

She had seen mission life and was not disturbed by the fact that dressing in style for missionaries meant whatever style people were willing to give you from their discards (the missionary barrel where people were known to put the missing half of the pair of shoes). The only thing which allowed most missionaries to buy new clothes was the gifts of benevolent friends and relatives.

Why was my wife not living up to my expectations and helping me out of this? As I said before, I still struggle with this call. But I do know that when God can't reach the head, He often speaks to the heart. When I wear myself down physically and won't admit my fatigue, my body will eventually get me the message.

My better half, my smarter half, my more spiritually sensitive half, my heart was not buying the argument that we could not afford this. She was determined to be obedient. She wouldn't let me off the hook that easily.

I came to recognize why Adam had failed. He tried the blame game.

God would not hear it then and He would not hear it now. I would have to

obey or disobey on my own. I could not hide behind my wife as Adam had

tried. God had given me the covenant of blessing for my home and that required my obedience. This was the role He had given Adam and now it was also mine. I could not blame the "woman thou gavest me." I could not blame my wife.

HOW DO YOU SPELL NEGRO?

On a warm day in Kenya, I was walking with a young white college student. We were on a dirt road which could become a mud road quickly with a quick flash of rain. An old Kenyan man walked up to us and started to exclaim in broken English how glad he was to see this young white man in his country helping him. He thought this young man was a fantastic blessing from the heavens dropped down by way of missionary airways.

I felt offended because the old man ignored me. After all, I was the young African American surgeon who had just completed four weeks of volunteer work in the nearby mission hospital. This man should acknowledge the fact that this short-term mission trip was costing me and my family about $10,000, not to mention the lost revenues from closing the office. What right did this white boy have crowding in on my credit!

As the old man turned to me, he said, "Oh and you....., you are a Ugandan!" I puffed out my self-righteous chest and exclaimed, "No! I am an African American!" He of course was not impressed with my red black and green nor my red, white and blue pride and went on to guess which Kenyan tribe I hailed from, all the time making me more irate.

Why couldn't this old man, who probably never had a copy of the New York Times or had not read Martin Luther King's Letter from a Birmingham Jail, understand what I was saying? "Can't you get it old man?!" I said with my body and spirit. "I am an African American. I am from the 'We shall Overcome, I Have a Dream, Red, Black and Green, Black Power, Kill Whitey Now, Muhammad Speaks generation of 'Say it Loud, I'm Black and I'm Proud' black Americans!'

You should be on your knees thanking God that one such as I has come to lift the white oppressors foot off of your neck and bring you the true Gospel of liberation in Christ! By the way, keep hope alive!'

The old man paused...., "oh.., you're a Negro!" he said.

Now, I'm really mad. Just where did this man learn such a word? What right did he have to use some colonial, demeaning, dehumanizing, slave term to me? I had come 8,000 miles away from home to be dissed by an old man who can't even spell Negro, probably.

Then the Holy Spirit stepped in. Don't you hate when that happens? He gently reminded me that He had called many European Americans to Africa and that many had given their fortunes, health and in many instances their lives to deliver the gospel. What right did I have to become offended because this man did not recognize my supposed common link?

If I wanted to claim something in common, I needed to share something in common as my white brothers and sisters had shared. Beauty is more than just skin deep when it comes to Jesus. It only begins once the Holy Spirit gets underneath the skin that we become beautiful.

When you look at it, we can't really blame white people for the attitude they have. They have been white a long time. They can't help it. For that matter you can't blame black people for the attitudes we have. We've been black (or colored, or Negro or some other name) for a long time.

How do you adjust your attitude in missions if you come from a culture which tells you are always right? How do you separate your culture from your Christianity? Because your nation has the most sophisticated army and the most influential media for entertainment, how do you separate that from your ministry in Christ? Americans believe that 'bigger is better.' Hence, typically when we find a problem, we are frequently inclined to spend more, supply more and build it bigger to make it better. We are not inclined to ask questions, when we already know the answers. We are not inclined to listen, as we are already talking about the next project.

We as black Americans have gone to the other extreme. When we see a problem in mission sending agencies which are dominated by white people, we kill the messenger and burn the message. We have been down so long that we feel justified in denigrating the messenger, even when the message might be right.

When we first went into mission work, the majority of our support came from white churches. It seemed many of the black churches didn't believe we would really go. Others thought; "Why should we support these guys who are going with a white organization?"

Now to the credit of my black brothers and sisters, I understand where you are coming from. I really didn't want any part of this either. However, God began to confront me and told me I was a closet racist. Of course I didn't believe Him. He obviously had misread me. He saw my actions, but didn't understand my heart. Maybe Hebrews 12:14 is inaccurate?

Then the Lord challenged me. He gave me an opportunity to get support in a predominantly white church in the Philadelphia area. I told the Lord, I was tired of going to such situations being the 'fly in the buttermilk.' I told God He needed to get someone else to do this. I told God it was not my job to go to such a place and tell people to do the right thing and take care of 'the least of these'. I don't really like those people anyway God.

Then the Lord said, "Racism? If they had refused to let you in, you'd come to me with great indignation. Now look at you!" Well, He had me...., this time...,at least for now. This church has proven to be our most generous and most faithful supporter. They have visited the work in Kenya and correspond with us on a regular basis. Okay, so God was right again. What do you want? He cheated. He already knew the answer.

I know that in order for us as black Americans to move forward in missions for the 21st century, we will have to learn from people whom we are not particularly fond of. I know that in order for white Americans to fulfill their part of the mandate, they will have to learn from people whom they don't think really know much about much.

We've been in our own way a long time. God has been God even longer. He doesn't just know the answer. He is the answer.

When I started out in this peculiar thing called Christian missionary work, I did not like the concept of being a missionary. I did not like the idea of being called a missionary. All I had ever known or seen of missionaries was old white men and women, carrying Bibles to dangerous, uncomfortable places to dangerous, undesirable people.

I had envisioned myself being prosperous and portulent (FAT and FULL). I could not imagine spending my life in a place not having access to a good theater, jazz and blues concerts, or good cuisine from a variety of places around the world. After all, how do you drive a luxury car in a jungle?

Where do you place your tennis court when you live near a swamp? What is the sense of having a nice tuxedo if it doesn't match the dinner attire of cowhide your host is wearing? Why should I put myself through all of this when there are plenty of senile, deluded old white men and women and even some crazy young white men and women, who are more than willing to suffer for the cause?

I needed a reason to avoid this calling. I needed a scapegoat upon whom I could cast this burden, someone to relieve me of my felt calling.. Someone unsuspecting. Someone willing. Someone whom I was not particularly fond of and who I could blame for the problems anyway. I found it in white people.

I had an excuse provided for me by those who blamed the white man for all of the evil of the world. If the Europeans and their new American counterparts had left the world order as it was, natural selection would have prevailed and the suffering and ignorance would have disappeared on its own.

It is indeed not my calling, but the white man's burden to carry the Gospel of Christ, because they owe it to the world for having made it such a horrible place. (You really need to have a MRI of your skull to see if your brain is there if you believe any of this drivel). Our experiences in overseas missions have all been in Africa. Suffice it to say, there has been and still tends to be some tension between some of our white brothers and sisters and their black coworkers.

Not only did we have break the color barrier in our own mission agency, but we have done so challenging some of the preconceived notions of who we are as people of African descent.

I was asked by one of my coworkers about the possibility of him a white man, leading a group of people from 'my race' whatever race that is, to Kenya as short term missionaries. I did not know how to answer him.

First of all, I had thought we were all of one race, i.e. the human race. Secondly, why did he not consider there were people of 'my race' capable of leading other people of my race on a short-term missions work? I bit my tongue and told him that there had already been two groups from our supporting churches, people of 'my race' in Philadelphia which had visited Kenya. They had made it back and forth across the big water safely without being led by anyone from 'any other race'.

Since being a missionary in overseas work, we have been made to feel welcomed by most everyone and I must add this with emphasis. I do know that the shock of having black people actually living, breathing and eating in such close proximity was a bit too much for some of those missionaries. I am not being paranoid in this.

We actually knew we were intruding in some situations as even the Africans were not welcomed at certain events in some mission homes overseas. Bible studies were held outside of one home, on the porch instead of inside the house. African children were chased away from the lawns and told to go home and not play with missionary children.

At one of our children's birthday parties we invited some of the Kenyan children to help us celebrate in a game with the prize being lots of candy. Towards the end of the game, I had one white missionary child scream at me and say "Tell the Africans to go home!" I trust she did not learn this in Sunday School. Our children were part of the integration work in the field. They were not aware of the unwritten policy that Kenyan kids were not allowed to play with mission kids on the compound. They invited the Kenyans to play at their birthday parties, the camp-outs at night and the basketball games.

One of my white colleagues wanted to integrate their children's Sunday School. When inquiry was made about how to go about this, they were told by one of the veteran missionaries of more than three decades on the field; "I think it is time to integrate." This was in 1996, after fully fifty plus years of mission work in this particular mission station. As I played Santa Claus at a missionary get together in December 1999, I was told by one of the missionaries that his three year old child was afraid of me because I was black. I found that baffling because practically every man around them was black. Who told her she was afraid?

Our experience in missions has included having some of our white brothers

and sisters, our own coworkers on the field, ask us about the necessity of allowing our African brothers and sisters, those people whom we serve, to use our toilets or drink out of the same glasses when they visited or worked in our homes. Traditionally in some circles we know, Africans were told to dig a hole for their 'doo-doo' and to use discarded cans and metal plates for eating utensils when visiting or working in the homes of missionaries.

Now to be fair, much of this could very easily be 'class-socioeconomic', educational and cultural differences. However, the effects are still the same. Integration is the difficult divide in America and it continues to surface even in missions in Africa. This is not an easy problem to eliminate by human efforts alone.

As far as digging a different hole for elimination of waste, I had problems answering questions like this, from our white coworkers. This was because I was still in the midst of recovering from America's legal apartheid and still effected by the unwritten race codes. I still shudder Every time the terms houseboy and housegirl are used, because of the connotations being made when calling a fully-grown person a child.

I have seen one missionary sit across the table in an official meeting and frequently teasingly slap a grown Kenyan man on the head. I know this same missionary would never suffer such indignity from this man, nor would they try it on a missionary coworker.

I walk along our compound and see young Kenyan women in attendance to young missionary kids and it reminds me of the 'Old South', where the black mammies tended and pampered white children of the privileged and left their own children unattended at home. I wondered how they must feel, these 'housegirls'.

In America today, no one with any heart of Christian kindness or political correctness dare refer to a black man or woman as boy or girl. Yet today in Kenya and I am sure in many parts of the world where missionaries serve, this is the norm. How do we build a people up in Christ if we continue to refer to them in demeaning terms?

This double standard made its way into the hospital. A missionary woman who would deliver a baby would do so in the operating room, with none but the very trusted Kenyans in attendance, behind screens and shaded windows. She would immediately be taken to the recovery room with a nurse in attendance for at least 24 hours or more. However, the average Kenyan was given no such treatment, giving birth in the crowded delivery room, little privacy, attended to by even the most junior staff. If the Kenyan mother needed a Cesarean Section for birth, her recovery was on the ward amongst the general population, immediately after the procedure.

I and my colleague Bob Wesche saw this double standard as unacceptable and argued vociferously for a recovery room for Kenyans who were operated on and an Intensive Care Unit for the very ill. After several months of badgering the nurses, missionary and Kenyan alike, I helped accomplish the goal of assuring that Kenyans having emergency surgery or critical illnesses were at least given a semblance of equivalent care of missionaries who underwent elective surgery.

I communicated my disgust to the Vice-President of our mission. I told him I felt betrayed. However, it was what I had expected. I had grown up believing that the term 'white Christian' was an oxymoron. But then I remembered, that I was not called by them, nor kept by them, nor called to serve in this mission's name. I was called by Christ, kept by Christ and called to serve Christ. I could not boycott my calling. I came to recognize that if indeed the call for missions was genuine, that this bit of racism was nothing more than a test, a challenge. The Vice-President was quick to write me a letter explaining this was neither mission policy, nor acceptable behavior by one of its employees. He further consoled me with words of apology and encouragement. Should I stay?

Could I forbear being slighted as I watched those who look like me being slighted. I know that even if I was not treated overtly the same, there must be some inkling of this that had to be suppressed when my white coworkers encountered me. Could I bear being treated less than equal for the cause of Christ?

Could I set aside my ego and my racial pride and let God use me in this

ministry even if I did not feel accepted? I remember telling the Lord that I didn't mind doing missions so much, but I just did not want to do it with these ultra-conservative, Republican, Bible thumping white folks. The Lord asked me then, 'who was the racist?' Was I too good, too righteous to work with these people?

Given all of these bad experiences, I know that without a doubt if these earthen vessels who were of European descent had not taken the treasure of Christ to these corners of the earth when they did, the Gospel may well not have ever arrived again on the African shores within this millennium (1900's). I say arrived again, because I have come to recognize historically that it has been there since the dawn of time. However, for this millennium there would be in all probability have been, no schools, no hospitals, no community health and development projects if my white brothers and sisters had not felt the urgency of meeting peoples' needs in Jesus' name in the deep interior of many of these nations.

Hundreds of thousands of children would not have been immunized, generations of mothers would have had no prenatal care, if these saints of a lighter hue did not go. Tenwek Hospital served a population of over one half million people. It was the only reliable source of health care for its 10,000 inpatients and 80,000 outpatients per year. Tenwek's ministry of Community Health and development has helped bring down the rates of deaths from diarrhea from hundreds of deaths per year to occasional incidences in far removed communities.

These statistics can be seen in many mission hospitals and institutions and it cost someone something. It cost a lot of white missionaries a lot. The cause of Christ has been advanced because of their sacrifice of their fortunes, health, comfort and often, very often, their very lives. So whose call is this anyway?

I am more and more convinced that we black Americans have missed our calling. Now this is true for many reasons. We have been denied access to mission sending agencies by design because of our color during the 19th through the mid 20th centuries. It has been documented that in the late 20th century in Kenya, the mission agencies actually conspired with the colonial government to prohibit African American missionaries from coming to Kenya.

We have had our own agencies limited in their outreach by our own government as we might have posed threats to colonial governments in some parts of the world until the mid 20th centuries.

We have had a mandate to put our own house in order as we fought and continue to fight for rights of humanity and citizenship in a land which continues to want to make us the "boogey man".

Whose call is it? No one can appreciate the oppressed people like those who continue to feel oppression. No one can speak to the suffering masses like the people who have suffered en masse.

Jesus is described as the suffering Savior in Isaiah 53.2, "he hath no form nor comeliness and when we shall see him there is no beauty that we should desire him." The bruised, hated, despised, ugly beaten badly savior, can speak to a world of people who identify with Him.

We represent a portion of the body that is held in dishonor. I believe that in America no people are hated and despised as much as the African and those of African heritage. When black/white couples marry in America, the children are automatically labeled as African American because white people will have no part of this mixed breed as their own. The blood of the African has contaminated the race and hence, it is no longer purely white.

This was actually a law, codified in Virginia. I can quote my daughter Christina on this as she wrote one of her 'white' friends;
The reason that interracial babies are to be considered mixed black dates back as early as the 1600, and to a law called the "one Drop Law" or the "Racial Integrity Act" that was formed in 1924. In 1664 Maryland banned interracial marriage due to questions over whether the offspring of a black slave and a white person would be considered a free person or property.

The "one drop law" simply put states that if any person had even on drop of black blood in them they were considered to be black. So the "one drop law" was not instituted with human beings, human rights, or the gene pool in mind, however it was a matter of ownership by slave masters.

It was about ownership of one person over another. However, slave-owners and many w whites at the time did not consider slaves to be humans with equal rights. When slavery was abolished by the 13th amendment in 1865 many southern states instituted what were knows as "Black Codes". In addition to stripping freed slaves of most of their newly acquired rights these codes continued prohibition of marriage between whites and blacks. This was based on a commonly held notion that Africans, and Native Americans as well were inferior races and interbreeding would pollute the white gene pool.

The one-drop rule is racist. It was historically implemented to create as many slaves as possible, and to make sure that no one crossed over to the "white community". This is awful for two reasons. First is that it implies that there is both a superior and an inferior race that we are not in fact equal, because if we are equal how can slavery be justified. And second is it prevents people from identifying with the totality of their heritage, since the creation of the one drop rule any person in America with any black heritage must be considered black and deny the white heritage and rights that belonged to them, that they could not take advantage of because of the one drop law.

I think that as long as people continue to put each other in boxes ex. Black, white, Indian, Asian, etc, we will continue to live with a divided mentality, and will have difficulty coming together as a people. And when we really get down to, and looked way back at our ancestor's ancestors whom of us are really 100% anything?

Few if any are. We need to spend more time embracing one another instead of labeling each other, because the same red blood flows through us all. Be careful about the things you say, especially when it comes to race relations. Many jokes are only funny to you, because you don't understand or respect the struggle. Then you come across as a bigot, who is also uninformed. I don't think you are a bigot, or a racist, I think there are things you may not understand, which is understandable. However, it's not an excuse to be carreless with your words or statements about other races.

Christina's observations and research have been very helpful in writing this book. She has the same fire in her belly as her grandparents and parents. We need to embrace one another, instead of labeling one another. The "one-drop rule" is the colloquial term for the standard that held that a person with even *one drop* of black blood was classified as an African-American.

The "rule" still influences the U.S. today—by de facto American color standards, a multiracial person with black heritage is considered black until they preemptively declare themselves otherwise--identifying, instead as white or Native American for example. The one-drop rule is a product of the American slavery system--it widened the pool of possible slaves, and reduced the possibility (horrifying to racist whites) that over generations African-Americans would drift into the white column.

It was codified in law in some places and held cultural sway in others. For example, as cited in the decision Loving v. Virginia. Virginia law (Racial Integrity Law of 1924) held that "Every person in whom there is ascertainable any Negro blood shall be deemed and taken to be a colored person, and every person not a colored person having one fourth or more of American Indian blood shall be deemed an American Indian; except that members of Indian tribes existing in this Commonwealth having one fourth or more of Indian blood and less than one sixteenth of Negro blood shall be deemed tribal Indians."

No one is despised in America and in much of Europe like the African and those of African descent. We have a testimony to share with a world of people who feel despised and rejected. We cannot wait for someone else to take this responsibility. Our testimony of suffering does not belong to us. We have a peculiar mandate to share our worldview in a way no one can do for us.

I find it interesting that Simon of Cyrene, the black man who carried the cross for Christ was there to ensure the crucifixion took place. Had this man not have been there, it is possible that

Jesus would have died on the streets of Jerusalem and not on the cross of Calvary.

I believe that the black man, those of African descent are just as crucial in Christ's return. I believe that somehow by not heeding our calling, we impede the kingdom in more ways than we realize.

We cheat the world of seeing a side of Jesus the Christ when we ignore our calling to be His ambassadors to the world. We cheat the world of seeing how the bruised and battered servant can still fulfill His calling. People know of our history. They will marvel at us if we can take Christ to them in the midst of our troubles. Anyone can share Jesus when they are on top of the world. Can we share Jesus when we are despised and dejected? Can we be the bruised and hated Jesus that Isaiah talks about? I believe we cheat the world of seeing a part of Jesus when we ignore this calling.

The apostle Paul declared "woe is me if I preach not the Gospel" (1 Cor: 9:16) and Jeremiah in 20:9 declared it was like a fire shut up in his bones. I believe that if we allow this fire to remain shut up in our bones, it will burn its way through some way. Much of the pain we feel as a 'black church' is because we are allowing this corporate body to smother the flames of the gospel in our lives. Much of the pain in our communities is there because we don't share our testimony with the world in need of seeing the suffering Savior.

We were either too embarrassed of our past and hence we had no future to be proud of as we tried to embrace the safety of the present. Or we idealized the past and saw no need to move towards the future, nor eternity because we had so many glories in the beautiful motherland.

Whose call is it anyway? It's your call Michael, or don't you know how to spell Negro?

IT COST MY WIFE/
NEGLECTING HER NEEDS.

I have never known her to cry that long. I felt helpless. When our kids were driven away for boarding school in Kenya for the first second time in September 1990, I saw a side of my wife that still shakes me. It was at least a five-hour drive, and we stayed behind, entrusting our kids to other missionary parents. Kay cried. We had driven them for the first trip, but this time, they were going away without us. We were obligated to stay behind and work.

She cried for more than eight hours straight. The following day she went to work. She wore sunglasses to hide her swollen, bloodshot eyes from her Kenyan and missionary co-workers at Tenwek hospital. I still wince at the thought of the pain she endured as she saw our kids driven away. My wife is God's second best gift to me.

I believe that if God had not heard my cry and sent me this beautiful woman, I would be in the same drunken stupor I was in the night the Holy Spirit came to me and revealed His salvation plan for my life which is my first best gift from God.

I was in my junior year in college at Lawrence University in Appleton Wisconsin. I had done all of the things that my mom had told me not to do, well at least many of them. I recall my mom crying too as she looked at me as I sat in a drunken stupor during one college visit she made to encourage me. College was such a lonely time for me. Appleton is a town in upstate Wisconsin. I had been told that black people were warned not to stay out late in the town. There was reportedly still a law on the books of the town that Black people could not stay overnight in town.

In the midst of my fear, loneliness and anxiety, I took to partying with the fellas. It took my mind off all of the reminders of my inferiority constantly around me. It didn't fix the problem, but it dulled its influence. No fraternities made us feel comfortable.

No societies or fraternities welcomed us. This was in spite of this being the mid '60's liberal, freedom era. The Lord God spoke to me one day in the midst of all of this insanity. He bade me open the Bible which my mom had given me three years earlier. He showed me in Psalm 1 that He could cause me to prosper. I told the Lord that I needed a soul mate in order to make it.

I told God that I could not be the kind of Christian He wanted me to be, unless I could have a woman that loved Him more than she loved me. He promised me that He would provide me such a woman. One and one half year later, I met Miss Sandra Kay Hugan in New Hope Baptist Church in Ann Arbor Michigan where I attended medical school.

This was not really love at first sight. It was more of my lust at first sight. Kay was a beautiful girl. I say girl because she was all of 17 when I met her. I could not take my eyes off of her. I was a freshman in medical school, dating a senior in high school. I even took her to her prom. I was afraid I would meet some of my classmates en route to the prom banquet. It was a challenge to both of us as I hid behind posts and columns at the hotel in an effort to remain incognito. I am sure she wondered if I was on some hallucinogen that night as I dodged real and imagined colleagues.

We were married two years later. Kay was attending Eastern Michigan University in Ypsilanti, studying accounting and I was in my junior year of medical school at University of Michigan. We now have more than 20 years of marriage and I find her even more beautiful and I love her even more.

I no longer hide when people come up to us unless I can't remember their names. She helps me then.

There were many nay sayers. Many in my family thought I was marrying 'beneath myself'. This was a young girl whose family had no professional people. She had never traveled. I introduced her to her first taste of something as common as Chinese food. That was considered a novelty. How were we gonna make it?

That was a good question. Our first year of marriage was a challenge. During the summer of 1977 I could only find work as a dishwasher in a restaurant, so we were on welfare for two months to supplement the income. My new bride had gone from the comfort of her mom's home to the life of a poor college student in less than one month. She was less than happy. What had she gotten herself into? When she became pregnant with Elijah a few months later, we had to depend upon government assistance for dairy products under the WIC (women, infant and children) program.

I was still doing some of the bad habits of hanging out with the fellas and this was not to her liking. Right away, she started to put her foot down. I had to determine my priorities. I think this is what I asked the Lord to do, wasn't it? Kay was an answer to my prayer. I began my clerkships in the hospital and Kay was full time in school. Right away, the mistress of medicine entered into my life. This mistress was so demanding that she would not even allow me the comfort of being at home without thinking of her. Medical school and the years which follow were some of the loneliest years for Kay.

I know she cried many times. I bought her a small puppy to keep her company and we named it Tasha. One day while we were away shopping, Kay got a sense of urgency to return to the house. When we got home we discovered Tasha had jumped from the porch with the leash and collar still on and had hung himself. Kay cried. My attempt at comfort had failed. I bought her another right away and we named it Dina.

Upon graduation from University of Michigan in 1979, we moved to Philadelphia in order for me to train in surgery. Kay had never lived away from home. We loaded up a U-Haul truck with furniture from my mother and some old pieces from our little place and moved. Elijah, our first-born was just about one year old. He got car sick in the truck just a few miles from Ann Arbor and Kay got upset because I wouldn't stop and take him to the doctor. In my typical male 'hunt it down and kill it' attitude, I rebuffed her and told her we had to reach our destination. Now in retrospect, I realize her real cry was that she was leaving home.

I was taking her away from all the comforts she knew. Moving was no big thing to me. We had moved over a dozen times while in Chicago where I grew up. Traveling to a new city was no big thing as we had traveled from coast to coast and made numerous trips to East and West Europe and Mexico while I was still a boy. I was insensitive to why she was near tears.

I was insensitive while we settled into a rooming house with a motorcycle gang living above us. I would leave for work at 5:30 a.m. and return at 8:00 p.m. the following day. Kay and Elijah were alone in that house with Dina. The surgical residency attitude is that 'the only thing wrong with every other night call is that you miss half of the good cases.' My mistress of medicine became more demanding and unforgiving as I needed to impress my seniors in order to keep my job and advance in the program.

I left Kay alone in Philadelphia. She had no job, no friends and she had left school mid-term to move to Philadelphia with me. She had left her college career, her family and all she knew to be with me. We finally made it out of that rooming house as Kay continued to cry in her loneliness. I needed to find a way to make my mistress of medicine get along with my wife. It is still a task I haven't mastered.

Over the next few months the strain on our marriage continued. Kay found herself getting lonelier and more in need of companionship. We moved to Sharon Hill and joined First African Baptist Church. Kay found friendship and fellowship there. Before she was finally settled, however, she got ready to leave me. She bought a plane ticket to return to Ann Arbor. She was so lonely I thought she would not survive our move and certainly our marriage would fail.

As she called me at the hospital (I was too busy to take her to the airport) and told me she was leaving I told her I loved her and would stay in touch. She told me that when she got to the airport she cried so much in front of the check in counter that she could not get the man to understand she had changed her mind. She says she knew if she had left, she would never have returned to me again.

(So she thought the move to Philadelphia was big...eh! What else do you have in store for this woman?). Kay stuck with me through my residency. She worked full time at St. Agnes Hospital in Philadelphia in the billing department and learned the medical insurance lingo and became proficient in medical terminology. She began to build her own life and came out from under the shadow of 'Dr. Johnson' as time went on.

Kay gave birth to Christina our second born in 1980 and then Emmanuel in 1983. She chose and bought our home in Upper Darby. As I worked overtime, double time, triple time to make the payments, I was rarely home for more than one day a week and then just for a chance to sleep and complain. Kay stuck with me. We never went anywhere for vacation during those years. I worked during vacation.

Kay would occasionally take the kids to Ann Arbor to visit family, but I would stay and work. At the end of those hellish five years, I told Kay I would take her on a vacation adventure of a lifetime. Zaire (now the Republic of Congo) was this adventure. It was not exactly the vacation she envisioned, but being a dutiful wife, she went along for the ride.

This was our introduction to missions in December 1984. We left the kids in the care of Kay's sister Brenda, who volunteered to come to Philadelphia for 7 weeks.

We had no prospect of a job upon our return to Philly. We had a few checks coming in from the work I had done which would cover the mortgage and groceries for those few weeks. We were heading to Africa!

Kay and I had a life changing experience. Our values and worldview changed. We had one thing in mind when we went. I at least thought I could do short term missions. Kay was just being a beautiful submissive wife.

We came back from Zaire and determined we would never do anything so foolish again. Missionaries in Zaire had to take everything for four years.

Four years of shoe sizes, corn flakes and toilet paper are hard things to calculate. We were determined that we had suffered enough from medical school and residency.

Why should we do anything like missions? I did not want to make my wife suffer anymore. I was tired of seeing and making her cry. I was determined to reward her for her faithfulness and her support all of those years. I would do anything possible to keep her happy. I didn't have to make her cry again. She made herself cry.

Kay showed a determination to love Christ more than she would love the world. She made a determination to love the Lord so much that she would give up her own aspirations to serve Him anywhere. In 1987 she heard the Lord tell her we needed to make another trip to Africa. I had heard Him as well, but I did not want to bring it up. I did not want to make her cry again.

Kay was determined to do God's bidding no matter what the cost.

We took our kids to Africa for the first time in December 1987. We served at Tenwek Hospital. It was here the Lord confirmed our call to missions. Kay used her skills she had mastered in computers which she had learned in putting together her physicians billing service in Philadelphia. She used her managerial skills she had honed as she managed my very busy private surgical practice.

As we returned from Kenya in January of 1998 where we had served for 7 weeks, we determined to close the practice. We sent all of our patients letters to tell them of our intended move. We sent letters to all of the referring physicians to let them know of our plans. We let our two office employees go. We sold some of the office equipment. Much of the equipment like computers and phones, we gave to friends and the church.

We began selling our house furniture and giving away clothes and toys. We gave away Kay's car to my mother. It was a car I had given her for her birthday. We made out our wills. The mission had made it known that we had to specify what we wanted done with our bodies should we die overseas.

It was the mission policy in the past to at least consider having the body buried on the foreign field.

What would we do if we or our kids were kidnapped? We had to prepare ourselves for this because it was the mission policy not to pay kidnappers. If we were held in some jungle in Africa that would mean, we would either be released or found by interested parties. To underscore this threat, we recently were required to have all of the family's hand and fingerprints placed on file with the mission.

We checked out our new insurance policies, life, health and dental. We resigned our positions on boards and committees. I sent notices to the hospitals that I was no longer going to be in attendance as a surgeon.

This move cost us a lot. It cost us friends as we were kicked out of one church because we were being more loyal to the mission than we were to the deacon's board and church choir and pastor.

I had not yet paid off my student loans, as I had the kids in private schools and was paying Kay's student loans, the house note and two car loans, not to mention two employees in the office. We went to Kenya with the mindset of using our residual savings to pay off the loans.

Because Kay was such a dutiful wife, I had tried to make life a little easy for her before this call. When she bought our home in Upper Darby, I let her pick it out. I wanted her to be happy. For the seven years we were there, she poured her life into this house. She had decorated, picked out the curtains, the matching towels for the bathrooms, the carpets and furnishings. She had chosen which flowers would be planted in which flowerbeds after the landscaping had been finished.

Kay had now decided that in order to do God's will for our lives, she was willing to do without. If I felt it was necessary to be obedient to the call to serve, she was going to go all the way. All the way meant ridding ourselves of the many things we called ours.

Kay either saw that it was sold, or given away. Since we did not have much time before departure, most of it was given away. I saw my wife give away her crystal glasses, her fine china and linens. I saw my wife roll up the carpets and take down the curtains.

I saw my wife give away the beautiful brand new bedroom set of furniture with soft lighting and mirrored matching dressers. I saw my wife give away her gold plated flatware and many of the wedding presents of small appliances and dishes. I saw her give away a lot of things, but I did not see her cry.

One of the things I had done before our decision to visit Kenya for the first time was to buy Kay a nice coat. I did not have enough money to buy her a full-length fur coat, so in the midst of my practice, I bought her a coat with a fur collar.

I still can see her cry as she accepted this gift years earlier. Now as we stood on the back porch of the house we had just sold, Kay cut the collar off of her coat. She wanted some memento of the good times. She was trying to salvage something of those good years. Now it was all gone.

Someone else, a Buddhist family was getting all of her good work she had put into the house. Someone else was using her fine china and flatware and crystal. Someone else was benefiting from her loss of so many things she had set her heart upon. She knew this and it made her cry.

Once again in Kenya, Kay did all the right things. She decorated the kid's rooms. She made them special treats. She put the labels in their clothes as they got ready to be driven away to school.

She tried to make each of Kenyan houses home, knowing that they would not be there to enjoy except for one out of every four months and for a brief visit one weekend out of every six.

I refer to these houses as homes because that is what happens. Each time we leave Kenya, we move out of and back into a home. The last house we lived in at Tenwek was in such bad shape, no missionary wanted to live in it. This was for good reason. The walls were in bad repair. The floor would shake when we walked on it giving the impression that the entire house would fall at any time.

The ceiling boards bowed downward as the rats overhead did the all night disco (could've been the music). Kay cried the entire first night of our move into this house. I had to assure her that we could fix the place up and after several doses of poison we were able to remove the rats which died in the open and tolerate those who died in the ceiling as the stench from their bodies slowly dissipated.

I often times feel I have neglected my wife. But God has given her such strength of character as to forget the things she left behind, that she has truly pressed forward to claim Christ. I have seen my wife 'count these things as dung' as Paul admonishes (Philippians 3:8 Yea doubtless, and I count all things but loss for the excellency of the knowledge of Christ Jesus my Lord; for whom I have suffered the loss of all things, and do count them but dung that I may win Christ.).

I have seen God bless her with an understanding of His grace and goodness that far surpasses all of the things she has left behind. This gives me cause to cry tears of joy.

P.S. As Kay reads this part of the story, she cries again. Being the sensitive guy I am I ask her; "Now why are you crying?" She says; "All that time, I never even thought you noticed my tears."

IT COST OUR CHILDREN AND OUR MARRIAGE

THOSE DUMB JOHNSONS

I often felt and I am still of the opinion that we have neglected our children for this work. I don't feel we always acted in the will of God. I think we acted many times out of our fleshly desire to see a work completed, or a project finished. We neglected our children in order to finish this work. It didn't necessarily have anything to do with Kingdom building. When we first went to Kenya as full time missionaries, we felt a great strain within our relationship with Elijah our first-born.

We had adopted the scripture 1 Peter 2:9 as our family scripture, where Paul notes that 'we are a chosen generation, a royal priesthood, an holy nation, a 'peculiar people'. From this was born our motto "THOSE PECULIAR JOHNSONS".

Elijah was not interested in being peculiar. He was 12 years old. He was coming into his own. The son of a successful black surgeon in suburban Philadelphia. He could see the writing on the wall. He was ready to be different but certainly not peculiar. Then mom and dad had to get this idea in their heads of going to Africa! Elijah would write letters and notes for us to find. Consider this letter for instance;

Dear Everybody;

The reason I hate being a Johnson is because I don't like being laughed at because I don't have any Nintendo game. And don't like having to stand in front of crowds. I don't like going places. I don't like being not able to see my friends. And I don't like missing field trips from going places. I also hate being the only person who has school at home until 5:00 pm, doing classes over and over. These are the reasons I am going to run away. I also don't want to be a missionary going to Kenya.

Elijah
p.s. I don't like my little brother.

Elijah would write letters about being part of those dumb Johnsons and deface our newsletters and prayer cards with the same words.

We were doing home schooling for Elijah as he was in 7th grade, Christina in the 4th, Emmanuel in 1st grade. Keturah was learning to get our attention with loud noises. Home schooling is a true test of your love of many things. Do you love your children? Do you like home? Do you enjoy reading and teaching? Mix the three together. It sounds alright when you see it on paper like this. But in reality it is worse than having your teeth itch. Just where do you scratch?

Home schooling in my humble opinion was created to punish people who did not appreciate their teachers when they were students. I think the worst lessons were those I had to teach on the 'birds and the bees'. I tried to make this an accounting and inventory course so Kay would be obligated to teach it. However, she refused to acknowledge that 'multiply and fill the earth' had anything to do with mathematics or stock management.

Our kids were hit with the double whammy of trying to do home schooling and raise support for missions on the road. We taught them from the back seat of the car and in hotels and motels as we spoke about mission in a variety of big and small churches in big and small towns. Elijah was not happy.

He would cut his picture out of our family portrait on the prayer cards. He was not happy. The other kids, being younger, Christina 10, Emmanuel 7 and Keturah 3 years, were relatively oblivious to all of this. They knew we were moving, but it didn't mean a whole lot to them. They just wanted to make sure we took all of their good stuff with them. Kay made sure of that. I am sure that to my estimation, at least 80 percent of that container we sent to Kenya had stuff like toys, kids clothes and the like in it (and of course the Nintendo). I could be wrong about this.

We made a covenant with the kids. We told them that if at the end of one year, if they felt collectively that this work in Kenya was destroying us as a family, we would come home. We made that promise and we were sincere in it. For the next two and one half years in Kenya, we never heard even a little discontent in their voices. The day they were driven away to boarding school, the day Kay cried so hard, it was traumatic for all of us. For several months we persevered.

Kay threw herself into her work in order to forget the pain she felt. I was always used to serving my mistress of medicine. Working hard and neglecting everyone and everything was normal for me. I don't think I gave it a second thought as I had grown accustomed to a tunnel with no light at the end of it. It is called surgery residency.

One day we received notice that we must keep Christina at home when she returned for semester break. The teachers and dorm parents were in agreement. Christina was depressed. One of them stated she was the most depressed child they had ever seen. We were not sure what to do. We did not want to neglect her emotional state. We thought we would have to do home school again. So we decided we would do whatever was necessary for Christina. After this break, Christina would stay at home.

God had another plan, however. At the end of that month, Christina appeared exuberant and revived and ready to return to school. It was God's grace in action. It was not the first time we would need God to intervene for Christina. During Christina's last year at boarding school, we received word that again she was in the dumps. Her counselor thought she was in danger of doing herself harm. Their advice was that we bring Christina home to Tenwek, or take her home to America.

Christina's grades suffered. Her relationships with her friends had soured. In addition, she was a terror at home whenever she would visit. It was a very heavy spiritual battle. The amazing thing about all of this is that we were oblivious to just how deep her depression was. Kay and I were so immersed in our work that we had failed to recognize our daughter was in trouble. We had neglected our calling to our children.

We were not able to be with Christina as she confronted a teacher who called an African student a nigger in front of the whole class. We were not able to comfort her when one of her teachers would tell her that slavery was a good thing from God and that the American Indians or Native Americans were allowed to be slaughtered in accordance with God's desire because they were an ungodly people.

These issues were handled by mail to the teachers and principals of Rift Valley Academy because we could never get away from work to deal with them. I never really felt totally satisfied at the outcomes. No teacher was ever disciplined or sent home for such insensitivities.

We hurriedly made the necessary move to get out of Tenwek when we finally recognized our failings in ministering to our children. Some personality and differences vision at our mission station awakened us to this. However, these conflicts served to awaken us to our missed ministry to our children. We moved to Kijabe hospital on the campus of the boarding school. This move was God's healing process in our family. It was His way of helping us keep our covenant with our children that the work of missions would not supersede our obligation to them.

As I write this chapter, Christina is doing phenomenally well in school, a freshman, studying pre-med with an eye to child psychology or psychiatry. She is more in love with Jesus than ever. She has blossomed to be the young woman that God promised us He could make her to be. Elijah is there with her in the same school, studying pre-med, a junior, with an eye to forensic pathology or plastic surgery (Go figure. Try to help the dead or enhance the living). He also likes his brother.

It took this same near meltdown to awaken us to the trouble continuing to brew in our own marriage. We were so intent on doing God's will through our lives, that we neglected God's doing His will in our lives. We placed all of our energies into doing and little attention was placed into being. We buried ourselves in work. I would average as much as five major cases per day. I would work two clinics on some days, surgery clinic, orthopedic clinic and do the consultations on the wards including covering for labor and delivery ward, doing the necessary casearan sections or difficult vaginal deliveries.

I would make rounds, operate and then try to lead a Bible study in the evening. I worked on several committees of Tenwek hospital, administrate as Medical Superintendent and try to keep up all of the correspondence with our 2,000 plus prayer and financial supporters.

I was working on a variety of projects including the internship program, the recruitment of missionaries from abroad, the intensive care unit, the intravenous fluid production plant for the hospital, the building of the library for the Tenwek primary school and providing books for that library.

I was frequently called upon to preach at the many churches in the area. I was the 'guest of honor' at a variety of special fundraising events. I attended weddings and funerals of my Kenyan friends in order to build our relationships, but at the cost of my own relationships within my family. In the midst of all of this, I would try to get to see our kids every third or fourth weekend by driving five hours away to their school.

I missed most of the ball games and special events they had. I would let Kay go to as many of these as she could. When we did come home to the US, I was not much better. I would work in order to make up the difference in the money I had not paid toward my student loans. I would visit any church which would request our presence in order to raise support and awareness of missions.

We would typically make at least two meetings every week. I would work part time, sometimes full time. In 1996 while at home, I worked full time as a surgeon, to help our kids get money for college. I studied for my surgical board recertification, published two newsletters, visited 30 churches, went to basketball games at the kid's school, made trips back and forth to visit Elijah in college and after 5 months of living like this, returned to work in Kenya exhausted and wondering what was wrong with God.

Little did I know that my relation with my wife was not improving. We were still in love, but we were drifting in our commitment to one another. Kay was no better when it came to overworking. She returned to Tenwek and immersed herself in work like never before. As Financial Comptroller of a hospital with a budget of over one million dollars, she was responsible for finding the holes in the pockets and the hands in the cookie jars.

With over 500 employees, Tenwek depends on donated professional help such as Kay. There are a lot of ways money could get lost. Kay did not make a lot of friends in that position. But she was able to make it possible for the hospital to operate on the income generated from patient fees. The capital development came from overseas still, but the day to day operation came from patient fees. Kay worked tirelessly with a staff that many of whom were not known for their honesty, efficiency or talents.

Upon her arrival in 1987, there was no one in computer services. She updated the hospital computer services to function for accounting and inventory. Upon our return in 1990, she oversaw the audits. She oversaw all of the legal and insurance needs of the hospital. She performed the audits for the outlying clinics and dispensaries. She monitored the cash and inventory books for the church bookstores.

These duties required her to spend hours on the road between Nairobi, Kericho, Nakuru and the dirt roads to the outlying clinics. She spent so much time on the roads that her duties at home and at the hospital would conflict. Home was easy to neglect as everyone understood, she was doing this for Jesus. It is just the way we lived. This all came to a head when we came to recognize that not only was Christina in trouble, but so were we.

We saw that we were not speaking of loyalty to one another, but loyalty to the work. If we did not have the wake up call provided by our work conflicts, we would probably have persisted in this madness. In Joel 2:25 God promised He would 'restore the years that the locust had eaten.' God has proven faithful. Our family, our marriage is stronger now than ever. God has fulfilled His promise.

Early on in our marriage we had begun reading the Bible together. One particular portion has been the solution to many of the problems we have faced. Deuteronomy promises that God would bless everything we put our hands to if we would abide in His will. We have also found that having a 'purpose' as a family has made a difference.

Our kids have never really complained about our work. They have been somewhat sheltered. They have gone to a boarding school, the Rift Valley Academy in Kijabe, Kenya. Keturah and Emmanuel did not really like the school. This school is an American 'oasis' in many ways. It has many of the trappings of any American school, with sports and entertainment activities suited for the mainly north American students. The school has many students from many countries and this allows our children to have a broad range of experiences and a broad view of the world.

Our children have experienced the best and worst of Kenya as they have gone with us to the slums of Nairobi and the resort hotels of Mombasa (at reduced missionary rates). To say they have missed something in the US is not true, unless one considers they have missed the opportunities to become involved in a culture which encourages them to desire more 'stuff' than they could ever use.

In April 1995, we made a Family Covenant. It is a document we have placed in our family Bibles and each copy of our personal Bibles. It is what we recite whenever we have our family devotions. It was conceived as our 'coat of arms'. The Johnson Family Covenant has helped Kay and me remember that our first call is to our God. We could be peculiar without being dumb.

JOHNSON FAMILY COVENANT

Our God and Father has given us life and health in order that we as a family may serve him and glorify him. We therefore resolve as a family that we will glorify God in our daily lives by

1. Representing Jesus Christ the Son of God, as we live and how we live.

   We will do nothing for self glory or selfish ambition, but in accordance with scripture 1 Cor; 10:31
   So whether you eat or drink or whatever you do, do all to the glory of God.

2. Bringing others to Christ by our deeds, words, thoughts, dreams and desires.

   We recognize the world is looking for hope in God and many will only read the scripture that they see written in our daily lives. In accordance with scripture Matthew 5:16

   In the same way, let your light so shine before men, that they may see your good deeds and praise your Father in heaven.

3. Living together in love at home and as a family.

   We can only do this by dwelling at unity at home as brothers, sisters, cousins, aunts, uncles, mothers, fathers, nieces, nephews, grandfathers and grandmothers. We recognize it is impossible to show love outside of the family if we cannot show it inside of the family. We also cannot love God if we do not love one another. In accordance with scripture Psalm 133

   How good and pleasant it is when brothers live together in unity.

We will share in rejoicing, sorrow, dreaming,
hoping, loving, losing, gaining, forgiving, laughing,
crying, success and failure. We will share one another's
burdens and victories. In accordance with scripture,
Romans 12:15 Rejoice with those who rejoice,
mourn with those who mourn

4. Recognizing that God will honor us as we honor Him.

   Our individual success must always be successes
   which will honor God.

   Those who honor me I will honor, but those
   who despise me will be disdained 1 Sam 2:30

5. Putting aside selfish aim and work only for the
   Kingdom of God, knowing that all of life's greatest
   needs will be taken care of by Him.

   Matt 6:33 But seek first His kingdom and His
   righteousness and all these things will be given
   to you as well.

A COVETOUS SPIRIT

I know that wanting things is alright. I have always desired a few of the finer things in life. I have never wanted to live in the 'lap of luxury'. However, a few of the good things would be okay. God dealt with me as I looked around and saw people who prospered in medicine and surgery as I wrestled with missions.

In the book of 2 Kings chapter 5, we meet a man called Gehazi. Gehazi was a servant to Elisha. When Elisha had healed Naaman of his leprosy, Gehazi secretly went behind Elisha's back to get some of the gifts Naaman had offered for the healing. Gehazi coveted the things of Naaman and was determined to get them even if it meant betraying the loyalty of Elisha. In receiving the gifts from Naaman which Elisha had refused, Gehazi felt he had made great gain.

In the world's eyes this is only natural to receive rewards on this earth for some good deed done.

We want what we feel we deserve, unless of course it is punishment for something we should not have done and then we want mercy. Gehazi was covetous of Naaman's gifts and he pursued him to receive it. When Elisha discovered this, he told Gehazi he would also receive Naaman's leprosy.

Whenever I return home to the US, I again enter into a world of temptations. It has been said that 'Opportunity knocks once, but temptation never leaves your doorstep.' Just ask Cain. In his jealous, covetous rage he sinned first in his heart and God told him in Genesis 4:7 'sin lieth at the door'. God goes on to tell him that sin wants to control him but that Cain can conquer it if he wants to. Cain unfortunately allows the temptation of jealousy to win and he sins in covetousness and then in murder.

As I allow the Holy Spirit to penetrate the selfishness of my own desires, I see indeed sin and temptation would like to rule over me. It comes in the covetousness of my own heart. I often reflect on how glorious my life would have been if I had stayed in the US and continued to build my practice. I have never known I could make so much money so easily.

As I have adjusted to making in one month what I used to make in one day, I am more than just disappointed at times. I look at the wealth others have accumulated. I look at the fine clothes they wear and the nice cars they drive. I hear them talk of their good retirement plans and their fabulous vacations and I become as covetous as Gehazi was of Naaman's riches.

I look at my colleagues as Cain looked upon Abel and would try to slay them in my own heart and mind. If I can't slay them physically, I would try to slay them spiritually.

This spiritual slaying is even more deceptive than the physical one. I can say in my heart; "Just who do they think they are? They have not sacrificed as I have! They have not given like me!" I can belittle them and their reputations in Christian circles and meetings with a smug expression of how good I am compared to them. This is murder of their reputations and characters.

There's a story told about a black American man who did not like fried chicken. Now that is a phenomenon in itself. He was well off. He had made a fortune. His fortune was made in, of all things, butchering chickens. Friends and colleagues were jealous of him because he had amassed such a fortune. They never recognized what it cost him, the love of fried chicken. (Many of you may think the trade off was not worth it).

Well, that may be a bit little simple story, but the illustration is good. We never know what it costs people to be where they are doing what they do.

When we covet their goods, we must also covet the burden that comes with those goods. I frequently wear a pair of sneakers which was given me out of the 'missionary barrel'. I was telling my daughter Christina one day that I got these sneakers for free. She replied, "Maybe they were free dad, but they cost you something."

I am proud of my friends and colleagues who have stayed home and succeeded in their practices. They have overcome tremendous odds to compete in these very difficult times of managed care. They have persevered when there are few visionaries or leaders to get us out of this moral morass. I admire them for their accomplishments and I applaud them for the fact that they continue to offer compassionate, competent care to many of the uninsured or under insured in our nation.

I do feel sad for those who are depressed for their state of being despite their successes in professional life. Jesus states in Luke 14:20 that we each must consider the cost of our choices. I am not sure that some of my colleagues really considered the cost of their choices. That is why so many of them are depressed and seriously wish they had not chosen medicine as a profession.

I know of some of my friends, surgeons, gynecologists and family practitioners who have quit their professions altogether. A recent article in March 1999 Time magazine tells of physicians who have gone into real estate, Amway and vitamin sales. The cost of college, medical school and starting a life thereafter have severely limited the choices they could make. The malpractice premiums, federal, county and city, taxes and fees including employee, business, professional fees, rental property, inventory and utilities make the cost of doing business prohibitive.

The various committees and professional organizations which each physician must join in order to substantiate credentials is overburdening. The peer review, chart review, ethics committees and residency reviews stifle one's life. The constancy of being on call and trying to be compassionate to one's patients (now seen as clients) and to one's family (now seen infrequently) is painful. However, this is the cost of being in practice in the United States today.

I believe that as a black American in particular that I have a particular obligation to serve the undeserved. I do not understand how anyone in general and black Americans in particular could quit the profession of medicine because of economic concerns. God has given us a gift that we could use to help so many people anywhere in the world. With the same determination we used to make it into medical school, we could make ourselves of use in other parts of the world.

We will be held accountable for this unused talent. As Jesus promises there will be much weeping and gnashing of teeth

(Matthew 25:30) . God expects us to use what we have so that we can acquire more. When we hide or bury our talents, we defy His command. We call Him stingy because He does not give us what we want as we want it.

Of course, being in mission work overseas has its costs. I don't want to imply that staying at home is easy, but it is a choice that is made and it does have its costs. I have seen what jealousy in my own life can do. It allows me to gloss over what it costs my colleagues in pain and suffering.

I am glad that God continues to deliver me from this sin of covetousness. I am kept single minded in the work I have before me by trusting God to provide for me in a way distinctly different in how he provides for them. We need each other. If it were not for people who stayed behind and earned money, I would never be able to go. Project MedSend is one example of a ministry which has allowed us to pursue this ministry and have others take the burden of paying off the remainder of my student loans. I was genuinely prompted to remain in the US and work to do this. The ministry would have suffered had Project MedSend not done this for us.

Covetousness and jealousy are sins God condemns because as they have rule and dominion over me, I cannot serve Him with a pure heart.

MISSIONARY KIDS OR HELL'S ANGELS

In my mind's eye I could see the headlines now. "Missionaries Hold Kenyan Workmen Hostage" It may be a bit of an exaggeration, but things frequently get blown out of proportion if missionaries are involved.

It was happening though. Right there on the Tenwek compound. The workmen huddled together and dodged the oncoming missiles hurled at them from the stone fence above their workplace. I wasn't there, but I can imagine the terror they felt.

"Incoming!" They all dodge for cover. "Did you see where it came from?" Says one worker to another.

"No I didn't. There seems to be at least two attackers involved. One of the missiles came from over...., Watch out! Incoming!" They both duck. The bright red colored missile has an amorphous and ominous shape which seems to change like an alien's body as it speeds towards the men hiding behind the construction site.

"Kapow! Splash" They are caught not by the missile but its contents. Fortunately the attackers are only filling the balloons with water. It could be much worse.

Kay and I get word of this only after the skirmish is over. The workmen come to complain to us that our son Emmanuel and Silas, the son of Daniel and Cindy Tolan have been involved in war games and it is interfering with their completion of work at the construction site. When the men tried to chase them away, the boys were less than respectful. Of course, being missionary kids they probably felt they owned the compound and anyone on it was fair game for their warfare.

When the men had reported it to their supervisor they thought the attack would end. However, Emmanuel and Silas were out to prove that America had integrated its forces and was now out to prove the superiority of this united front. In order to get revenge on the men for reporting on them the boys sneaked back sometime when the workmen were away and buried their tools. This of course did not do well for negotiating an end to the war. We had to make the DMZ (Demilitarized Zone) begin at our front door and extend to the Tanzanian border. The truce has held since then.

I tell you this war story only to emphasize that Missionary Kids, or MK's as they are known are not angels. They were never called to be missionaries. They are just kids and like any other kids, they are supposed to goof off.

Kay has taken great pains to remind me and everyone else of this. I often take offense when I am up 'preaching' about missions in a church and my kids are goofing off in the back of the church or auditorium, making me look bad. Kay reminds me that they have only heard this speech one hundred times this year and the reason it appears they are talking is they are really miming the words as I say them. I shoot back, 'They should at least laugh at my jokes!' Her reply; 'They did the first 30 times, so leave them alone!'

As Kay says these kids are not missionaries, they are just kids. "We are the missionaries, they just got drafted while we got called" The next time you see an MK remember this. It will make the moms feel better and maybe quiet their dads.

A CURSE TO ALL AROUND

I have searched the Bible over and over trying to find a way to get out of missions. There must be some secret word I have not found yet. I don't really know how to say this, but part of my being in Christian overseas missions is I don't want to be a curse to my family. I don't believe God operates on a tit for tat basis. I know that He is above that kind of thing. I don't believe God is sitting up with a scale seeing how much I have done and not done. I do know that Jonah tried to find a way out of missions.

Jonah didn't want to go to a people he figured were deserving only of hell. Jonah felt the situation was hopeless at best. The people were not of his kind.

They were not worth saving. We live in such a dilemma as this. We get angry at the terrorists of different sects or religions and when the thought comes to us that they might go to hell without Jesus we are prone to think; "Well, maybe that's where they belong!"

There may be some hesitancy in saying the final 'amen' with fervor when it comes to praying that God would keep that uncle or cousin from going to hell, knowing that he still owes you a lot of money, terrorizes your daughter and wrecked your car when you loaned it to him. "I don't understand how you could 'so love the world' Lord and I'm having trouble with loving uncle Joe!"

There are such people of the world with anger towards us for who we are and what we have. We can ask God 'how he could so love the world, when we have trouble loving our unruly uncle.' They are in need of the Savior and we don't want to go to them. We don't want to go because often time we feel hell is what they deserve.

I didn't want to miss the blessings of God. I don't want my family to lose what God has in store for me. I certainly don't want to be a curse to my family. I look at Jonah and I see that he became a curse to all of those on the ship. I wanted to avoid sinking the ship that is my home.

I am now living in a house provided through the generosity of a supporting church. So far they haven't sent me a utility bill. I don't know if they forgot to, but by the time they read this chapter it will be too late to collect. Anyway, they also gave us a car. They paid for the transfer of title so we could meet with our supporting churches in Philadelphia and beyond without using up our own limited resources.

Our two oldest children are in a college with a tuition bill which is per year a multiple of our salaries over several years. Our two youngest children's tuition in school is just under our monthly salary. God has provided in a variety of ways, the means for these needs.

I am working part time and it is tiresome. Even in this fatigue, I see God's benevolence as He gives me days off to write this book of memoirs. The boat is sailing steady. No storm is raging. I am in no danger of being thrown overboard. God has provided that I am not a curse in my home, but a blessing. I haven't been swallowed up by any big fish.

In point of fact, we are in deep water bringing up big fish as God has filled our nets with an overabundance. In addition to all of these blessings, God has allowed me to see a great deal of success in my own Nineveh. I have enjoyed the ministry of Men's Bible study while at Tenwek and Kijabe hospitals. I receive letters frequently from men who participated in those studies, thanking me for taking the time to impart them with a different view of the faith.

Also, in keeping with Bible instruction, I aided in the development of a project that began a men's prison ministry so that hopeless men might find new life in a situation where death may have been preferable to the old life. Christ sets people free.

The building of the partnership for internship for mission hospitals was a tremendous encouragement. I was very much instrumental in beginning this in the mission hospitals. As the interns work in these church hospitals, they are seeing Christ work through committed volunteers who have left their homes to obey a call. There is no doubt that they see Christ being lived out and this serves as an inspiration and encouragement for them to do likewise.

I am excited about the family medicine residency which I pursued despite the nay sayers, as I see it coming into being. I now know that because of Kay's and my efforts, the mission hospitals have hired at least six Kenyan physicians who were former interns.

I have seen within my lifetime the effect of persistent effort and how this effort is transforming the face of personal in mission hospitals. I have been tremendously blessed in Nineveh.

TASKER STREET BAPTIST
CHURCH A SAFE PLACE TO HIDE

We had lost the privilege of worshiping in one church because of what was perceived as a lack of loyalty on our part. We felt called to missions. The leadership felt otherwise. As we prepared for missions, it was near impossible to convince the leadership of our calling. We lost our 'membership' and in the African American church, a deacon without a church home is like a lost soul. He will not find a warm welcome in the immediate Baptist community as word spreads of his disloyalty. We needed a place to call home. We found it in the fellowship of Tasker Street Missionary Baptist Church, in south Philadelphia.

In a world of the local church, many black American Christians find their whole definition. They can be chairman of the board of an auxiliary. They can be president of a certain guild. Losing these positions of influence in their fellowship is a blow because so few of them have any positions of influence in the world. Historically most of them have worked at low end and dead end jobs. The church offered them identity and status.

Before the American Civil War, black freedmen and women as well as their offspring, could frequently only document their emancipation by certificates of baptism. Going to church meant more than just finding spiritual freedom, but literally physical freedom. Black men and women once freed, would owe allegiance to the church in a particular town, and not wander too far from that town, as to do so risked their freedom as such certificates could be destroyed by any 'slave catcher'. The higher up the ladder one could climb, deacon, usher, Sunday school teacher, pastor, etc., the greater the prestige. The pastor held and still holds absolute sway in many if not most of the African American churches.

We chose to ignore and forego these positions and privilege, places of perceived safety. We cannot stay in the safe place, because it is not really safe. Our love for Jesus must surpass all other loves. Our love for His will must surpass anyone else's will for our lives, be it mother, father, sister or brother as Christ expresses in Matthew 10:37.

We are proud of Tasker Street's hunger for missions which is becoming more evident every day. God has used this church as the balm to heal the wounds of rejection.

It is important to recognize that most African Americans who are interested in overseas mission work are ignorant of what exactly this entails. I had never met an overseas missionary in any of our churches in my more than 20 years of being a member in black Baptist churches. I was ordained a deacon, taught Sunday school, worked with inner city mission projects to public housing projects, visiting the sick and giving communion to those who were housebound.

As we looked for an encouragement for our calling, we got none from our pastor. In point of fact, we got very much discouraged. As Jim Sutherland posits in his survey of African American Missionaries (AFAM); " Pastors are conspicuous for their near-absence in motivating into missions any of the survey population. Of all the 102 missionaries, only six percent were motivated by their pastor. Only five percent of the 102 were motivated by the local church or a church member. The church, then, can only be considered a dis-incentive to global missions, in distinction to being even of no influence. "Therefore, a strategy to awaken the AFAM church must focus upon an awakening of the pastors".

EATING FOOD THAT DEFILES

We are invited out for dinner. We should probably bathe first! No one who has worked all day and is invited out to dinner at one of the prominent people in the community would dare show up sweaty and dirty.

It was our first visit to Tenwek and we wanted to leave a good impression on our host for the evening. I decide I will take my bath first. I start the water in the tub and go to get a towel from the closet. I come back to the tub and look in it with disgust and awe. "Kay! Kay! Come in here! Quickly!"

Kay runs in expecting me to have cut myself fatally with a razor or something only to discover me standing over the tub looking down.

"What is that' she says with equal horror?

"It is my bathwater!" I shout back.

"Are you gonna get in that?"

"I don't know. I don't feel that dirty!"

The water in the tub is filled with silt. It has the color of a very murky tea. It is probably two-thirds water one-third dirt. This was the condition of the water when we first arrived at Tenwek Hospital in 1987. We marveled that when we made ice cubes there was a kind of moving hologram of dirt in the center of the cube, which never froze completely because of this contaminant. Great conversation piece right now, but back then it was a bit offensive.

It called to mind our afternoon teas in Zaire just four years earlier. It would be mid-noon, maybe 95 degrees Fahrenheit. The host would bring us scalding hot tea to cool us down. They would set a nice big bowl of sugar in front of us teeming with sugar ants. Everyone ignored the ants and took two large teaspoons of sugar and put it in the hot cup of tea. The ants of course would be instantly boiled and rise to the top of the cup where they could easily be scraped off. I know veteran missionaries who would just leave the ants in for the extra protein. Cookies are hard to come by in Zaire.

Back to the bath. I put my foot into the tub of warm water and it disappears in the silt. "I can't even see my foot! I definitely don't feel that dirty" I say, "lets just go to dinner.

It was just as well. The walk to dinner was 'just here' as the Kenyans like to say. 'Just here' usually means within the district or less than a ten mile journey. If it is 'a little further' you must decide to either drive or stay overnight. If it is 'a long way', you need to plan on letting your friends and relatives know when you might come back and take your passport too. Remember these terms if you head to Kenya.

We walk to 'just here' and after one half hour of jumping over streams, fences, walking over meadows and through bushes and over rocky trails we arrive 45 minutes later. The kids are worn out. It is dark outside about 8:00 pm. We are sweaty and ready to go back. It is just as well that I did not bathe.

Our dinner has been prepared and the places are set at the table. Just what am I getting my family into? I must be a good example for them. Leadership has its costs!

It really didn't smell bad. If it only looked familiar, I could probably swallow it without a problem. If the lighting were better maybe I could find something in it that I could trust to put in my mouth. It looks bad under the dim light of the kerosene lamps. It smells funny, but as I said, not bad. I know there is no running water (except the water they run down to the stream for) for them to wash their hands in preparing the food. I've seen the flies around the house. I've seen the cow dung in the yard.

I've seen the scrawny chickens running around the yard with the even scrawnier dogs. I found out later that the chickens are older than the dogs which accounts for the determination one must use when taking a bite out of a drumstick. The dog would probably have been more a more tender selection.

I'm sure there must be a Biblical way to avoid eating this food. The host set it in front of me. I wish he would not have been so generous. He cuts me a big chunk of this stuff. It looks like a block of semi-dry cement. It is what is known as ugali in Swahili. It is pronounced like, oooh-golly. I am thinking oooh-golly, do I have to eat this?'

The staple food for Kenyans is this corn meal mush. You can invite a Kenyan to your home and serve him a one-pound steak and two baked potatoes, several plates of vegetables a generous desert and enough tea to fill his bladder. But unless you serve him this ugali, he feels he hasn't eaten.

They have a more fluid version of it in the morning which is a porridge and then in the afternoon, there is ugali. You can eat ugali and cabbage or cabbage and ugali, or any combination thereof three times per day, seven days per week, 365 days per year that is if you are fortunate enough to eat every day of the year.

So how can I turn my nose up at a meal like this? Is there a Biblical precedence for turning down this food. Jesus did say something about food defiling the body..., or was it the heart which defiled? Was I afraid of getting sick from eating the food, or was my own pride and ego as Jesus relates in Matthew 15:11 which was defiling me. What right do I have to be a picky eater?

It was not the food which defiled, but my attitude towards the food. My attitude made me feel like vomiting, when my stomach might be waiting to take it all in? I close my eyes and say the standard missionary prayer before eating a foreign meal; "Lord, I can get it down if you can keep it down!"

I didn't know not to eat it all up. Okay, here it goes! One small step for man..., in goes the first spoonful and the bolus of ugali sticks to the roof of my mouth and my tongue and teeth work to moisten and soften the ball of food. I force the mass towards the back of my mouth and I notice that the more I chew the bigger it seems to get. Okay, let's swallow before it gets as big as my head! Going..., going..., gone! Uh oh! It wants to come back! I grimace a bit and stifle the urge. It goes down again but not without much protest from the awaiting intestinal villi. As the cold sweat beads on my forehead, I begin to realize this is going to be a long night.

As I finished my first helping, my host, in a desire to show his generosity, shoveled more on my plate. I, in my ignorance, ate it all up. He in his generosity, filled it again, for the third time. Now I'm curious; 'Is this some kind of game?' I know that if I eat one more handful of this stuff, (there were no spoons), they will have to bury me here. So I looked up at him as he stood over me threatening me with that spatula full of ugali. I pleaded with him not to give me anymore. He smiled because I was finally full and that is every Kenyan host's objective. They are a generous people. I thought to myself; 'this is a bargain..., all you can keep down for less than a dollar!'

This generosity persists in many homes, despite the fact that they will often have to neglect feeding their children in order to accommodate an uncaring guest such as myself.

I felt like I had just swallowed about 5 stones the size of soccer balls. As the food hit with a thud my life began to pass before my eyes. My belly began to stick out and I could feel my gut trying to figure out whether it should move this food forward or backward.

To be kind, my host now brought me some mursik. That's what is called. It is pronounced 'more sick'. That is just what it did to me. To me it is really kind of yogurt of an unusual blend. I hate to say much more than this. Mursik is made by placing milk in a charcoal coated gourd and allowing it to sour. When it is at its peak it is considered a fine delicacy. Mursik I am sure must have some vintage qualities to it (this could have been a Bomet '85 year, one of the finest). I have since learned that the charcoal is also sometimes added as a cathartic (induces diarrhea), an anti-emetic (inhibits vomiting) and an antacid. I am not sure if I should term it an exotic drink or untraceable poison.

I tried to get out of this one. 'I can't drink milk!' I told my host. 'Haven't you ever heard of lactose intolerance' I then went on to explain the enzymatic deficiency which only manifests itself later in life and on special occasions such as when one is served Mursik. As he listened, he poured the Mursik smiling, almost sinisterly at me all of the time. 'Plop, plop, dribble, plop' it came out of the gourd into my glass. It kinda looks like dirty snow slush, even has those little pieces of charcoal in it like the pieces of tar in the slush. I put it to my lips and stifled my urge to vomit. It smelled like cottage cheese gone bad. I wasn't sure I would be alive to tell this story after this delicacy.

The walk back home seems even longer. If only we could call a cab. That night I lay awake as my intestines tried to pass the bolus of ugali mixed with mursik. My body decided it would not pass if forward and it was too far downstream to bring it back, so it just laid there and fermented some more.

As I lay there thoughts brewed in my mind. Kenyans are such a generous and kind people to us. Whenever I visit a home, no matter how poor they may be, they make the extra effort of sharing with me. It may be their last and their best, but they will share it. The chicken that man shared with me was the equivalent of going a night out on the town in one of the finest restaurants in America. He shared his best with me and did it not because I deserved or respected it. He shared his best with me because he wanted to show me kindness and love. Isn't this what Christ would do? In my desperation not to defile my body, God revealed how defiled my heart already was.

The next day I decided that henceforth I would learn to say enough and mean it. But I also learned, the defiling moment for me was my own attitude towards my host's generosity and kindness. I lived to have another meal.

FRAGILE FLESH

As I sit here today I realize that the work we have before us is formidable to say the least. We have set out on a course to help Kenya be all we feel that it should be. Note what I say. It is not necessarily all that God would have it to be. We missionaries have it set in our minds that somehow within our fragile fleshly frames, God has entrusted us with the vision for the nation of Kenya.

There may be some truth to this. God has used some vessels of low esteem to do some mighty things. He even used an ass to speak to Baalam (Numbers 22:22), so He can certainly use an American missionary. The challenge I find is not so much to be used in mission work to evangelize for Christ. The greatest challenge I find is how to allow God to do His work in my own life. I am reminded that, as one pastor put it, 'I do not use the power of God, but the power of God uses me.'

I find so many missionaries returning to the field having no vision of what God is doing in their own lives, but ready to tell the Kenyans what God can do in their lives. How can God use me to minister to others if He is not already ministering to me? I personally know of at least one missionary who confesses returning to the field because being at home is uncomfortable. I know of others who don't confess such but have the work ethic which proclaims it.

It becomes more and more apparent to me that God is unwilling to use me if He has not at first prepared me for the work and given me a definite work to do. If there is no work to do, I should stay at home and get a job.

The day I received my confirmation by the American Board of Surgery that I had passed part two of my boards, I received by phone my interview and acceptance by the board of World Gospel Mission. It was a confirmation that God would not send me to the field unqualified to serve Him in the capacity to which He had called me. God did want me to be at my best.

I had thought that being a missionary surgeon meant that I could get away without being my best. I could show up in any type of clothing because most of my patients had dirty, ragged clothing. I could avoid punctuality because that is what people expected as they were not time conscience.

I did not have to study to 'show myself approved' as 2 Timothy 2 admonishes because when it came to the Bible I already knew more than anyone else in the Bible study. I did not have to have a clear distinct call, because people there wouldn't know the difference in me one way or another. I could allow my personal, professional and spiritual life to be undeveloped because I was after all working in an underdeveloped part of the world.

This was part of my fragile fleshly nature. My ego would conflict with the Holy Spirit. I would walk after the flesh and not after the Spirit as admonished in Galatians 5:16. The pride of life had seized my every thought. I began to think I could do all things without ever considering the consequences. Part of feeling this way of course was because I was so frequently called upon to do all things.

I was sought to minister in areas for which I am completely unprepared. I took on more than I should or could and I burned out. However, there was no one else there to do it. In my desire to help, I developed my own standard of counseling and caring. This fragile flesh, this earthen vessel began to think this standard was the spiritual standard.

After a period of three months of being on call for every night, followed by several months and years of every other night, I began to recognize my vulnerability. I began to hate the people I served. I am a fragile fleshly frame. I did not want to see another woman in obstructed labor, another bowel obstruction, open hip fracture or depressed skull fracture.

But if God could use Baalam's ass to speak to him, He could certainly use me in my fragile state to give a testimony of what He has accomplished in my life. Maybe that is what being fragile is all about. I am the foolish thing which God is using to confound the wise.

I am the weak and discarded vessel that God chooses to place the treasure of His light in to help others get a vision for missions.

WHEN YOU HATE THOSE WHOM YOU SERVE (AKA BURNOUT)

It has been a long day. The clinic is full of patients still. The number of unanswered consults on the bulletin board keeps increasing. There are cases from yesterday not yet done. There are sick people in the ward not yet seen. I haven't seen my children for several months. I don't have any vacation days left.

I get a letter that I have defaulted on my student loans and I don't have any money to buy my wife a gift for her birthday. I am tired. I am ready to call it a day. My last patient's wife is crying because he has AIDS and it is obvious that he has passed it on to her and her newborn child.

He is dying on the ward in spite of the fact that I risked my life operating on him for bowel obstruction. She can't pay his hospital bill and doesn't understand anything I am saying to her in Swahili which is being translated to Kipsigis.

I know I am supposed to be understanding. I know I am supposed to be compassionate. I know that I can't even begin to meet her emotional, spiritual, psychological or financial needs. I know

I should love this lady in the Lord. I know I am supposed to "cry with those who cry and mourn with those who mourn", as Paul admonishes in Romans 12:15. But somehow, I have begun to hate her because she now asks, 'Doctor Johnson, can you help pay my husband's hospital bill?' I have begun to hate her because she and everyone like her is sucking the life out of me!

I go home after my 12-hour day. I get there to find the clothes are washed by our house helper. The clothes have been neatly folded and left in a pile sorted appropriately. This pile for the kitchen, this one is for the bathroom. This is linen for the dining table and these are sheets and these are children's clothing and on and on.

It slowly becomes apparent that the house help is stealing clothing items for themselves. This is of course the sorted pile you don't see; i.e., one for thee and two for me. I have been contributing to this man's children's education. I have been giving them clothing and shoes and socks. I have helped them build their house with building materials and bought them a cow for their families' farm.

I have preached in the church in their home village and given donations for the building fund and Bibles and Sunday School materials. And this is how they treat me! Why is he stealing from me?

My anger is interrupted by a knock on the door. It is someone carrying a note from a nearby church pastor. They are upset with me because I did not give them all of the money I had promised for the Vacation Bible School.

I explain to the messenger that I had given exactly as I had promised and that was all I intended to give. He goes on to explain the note further, defensively adding that "Dr. Johnson, people are not trusting you at your word because of this."

At this point, I am thinking "Where can I get my hands on some napalm?"

The disciples did this one before I did. They asked Jesus if it would be alright if they could call down hell fire to destroy the town of people who refused to hear their message (Luke 9:54) They told the children that the master was too busy for him to spend anytime with them. They wondered why Jesus would spend time with prostitutes, drunkards, swindlers and liars and people whom they were supposed to hate.

They must have been upset with all of those hangers on. First it was the creepy little kids who needed to be touched and blessed by Jesus (Luke 18:16) and then all of those people begging for bread (Matthew 15:33).

It is easy to hate people whom you are called to serve, especially when they interfere with your version of the kingdom. In the midst of my busyness, this lady was asking for more compassion and understanding. She wanted something of which I had no more. She wanted me to give money when I had already sacrificed money.

She wanted me to give time when I had no more time. She wanted me to risk my health to save her husband which I had already done. I felt like I was short of breath and there was someone sitting on my chest while someone else was sucking the air out of my lungs.

The church leaders came to me one day after I had finished one 12-hour work shift in a 70-hour week. I was working as medical superintendent, writing, editing, re-editing the Tenwek Hospital Annual Report. I was taking call every other night and when my surgical partner would take his weekend off, call was every night.

I was setting up the Continuing Medical Education program for the nurses and other clinical staff. I wrote the lectures and gave the lectures to the nurses for the first two years of my stay at Tenwek.

Every other consult on the ward was an emergency. Every other consult from the outpatient was something I had never seen before and did not know how to manage. I had become the neuro-orthopedic-urologic-gynecologic-plastic surgeon of Tenwek hospital. I'd only wanted to give my all to Jesus, not do it all for Jesus.

I was tired of setting fractures, putting on casts, putting in hip prosthesis and even pacemakers under poor x-ray control. I read my own x-rays and ultrasounds. I did vacuum extractions of obstructed labor, sutured lacerated corneas, removed foreign bodies from the eyes, performed bronchoscopy, colonoscopy, cystoscopy and esophago-gastroscopy. I didn't like having to teach anesthesia at the same time as administering anesthesia. I had only learned to do a spinal myself and intubating after paralyzing a patient still scared me.

Making the right diagnosis of a particular tumor took at least 4-6 weeks as the pathology would be that long in coming back. Trying to make the right decision clinically was often just guesswork.

I could not believe these guys were telling me I was not giving enough of my time or ministry money to their local congregations. We had supported Vacation Bible School, bought Bibles and study aids. We had transferred money to put roof on church buildings and dig wells. We had helped with the education fund of students in the church and transferred thousands of dollars for the needy people fund within the hospital.

I began to feel used and abused. I had never been approached by the local church to ask me about my needs. When I would lose a patient, no one asked me how I felt. When I was stressed about my children's state of mind or performance in school or behavior, no one from the church came to minister to me. Yet when they wanted more from me, they felt bold enough to write and send delegations to alert me of my shortcomings.

Hating those you serve for me meant it was time for me to leave Tenwek. However, there was nowhere to go. The only way out when we first arrived at Tenwek was the horrible dirt road that leads to nowhere, or further out there was a resort town of Kisumu. Affording the time and the money were two things it was hard to do at the same time. It reminded me of my surgical residency.

Every trip to visit our children took away our vacation days. Every trip to visit our children cost us in travel money as we had to pay mileage on the car and find a place to stay either in a Nairobi hotel at $60-80 per day, or on the school campus at $10 per day. It was a five-hour drive on a good day, if the road and car held up. We would return from such a weekend and return immediately to work on Monday. This was not fun. And it was all of these people's fault. I began to hate them. They were the cause of all of my problems. The only way to make them leave me alone was to ignore their calls and complaints.

Burn out started to show in how I treated my patients. I would make rounds late. I would respond to calls with less than urgent pace. I would hide myself in the house with the curtains drawn and hope no one would visit or call.

Making rounds had become a twice a week affair. With as many as 30 to 40 patients on the ward and averaging four to five major cases daily, I was losing my perspective on life. I no longer even considered people as people. They were just procedures that needed to be done. I didn't want to talk to them, I just wanted to do whatever procedure needed to be done and see them a few days later and pray they made it out of the hospital before I could learn their names or get too close to them.

It is at this point the Holy Spirit must remind me that giving is possible without loving, but loving is impossible without giving. I was interested in giving without loving. I was angry. I had begun to hate the people I was serving.

I now know that unless God gives me strength to carry on, I

can never serve without hating the people I serve. I can never love them. God has to love them through me.

ROSA PARKS,
PLEASE COME TO BOMET

First of all, "Lord, why did you send this city boy who was born and raised in Chicago, had spent the last ten years of his life in Philadelphia to this place that is not even a speck of dust on the map? What did I do wrong Lord?"

Bomet is where we found ourselves permanently stationed in 1990. I almost want to say condemned, but that would be a bit too depressing. If you were to visit there, however, you might think otherwise. As you walk the 'streets' of Bomet the thing most striking is how much it resembles a town from the early 1400's in America. The only sense of order in the town planning is that the buildings are in straight lines.

There are a variety of buildings lining these streets. The surface of the streets is nothing more than gravel and dirt. Deep ruts caused by the heavy rains have unearthed stones as the mud is washed downstream. A visit to the bank in Bomet during our early days there, was best made on a sunshiny day as it was near impossible to count the money if the sky was overcast. This is because, there was no electricity and hence only kerosene lanterns in the bank.

Walking down the streets you see people gathered in groups discussing a variety of topics. Town gossip, politics and of course farming issues are very important. Too much rain, too little rain. Too much sun, too little sun. Why did the government sell us bad seed? Why does the government buy our crops so cheaply from us and sell it so high on the open market?

Cows and other livestock also congregate. Of course these animals are not house trained and do not know there are appropriate places to relieve themselves. You must be careful where you step in the streets as you might be gored by a cow or jostled by a herd of sheep and goats.

Boys and girls can be seen running up and down the roads in town. Most are clad in ragged, dirty clothing and some have shoes. They play just like kids all over the world. They laugh and smile at us. They kick an old empty can and home made soccer balls, made of old plastic bags and strings.

There are some bars and restaurants and a myriad of general stores. You can go into these stores and buy the much needed necessities, seeds, fertilizer, barbed wire, dish soap and even spaghetti. No spaghetti sauce is available, but you can buy spaghetti.

We had to learn Swahili. It was a good thing to do. If you are going to communicate with people, knowing their language sure makes it easier. We took advantage of this, not because we really wanted to, but our mission demanded it. So of course, we complied. I actually enjoyed learning a new language. It was a source of contention in our marriage as I had to force Kay to learn vocabulary and study. After a few days of class she refused to speak any Swahili, at least not to me. When I think on it, she wouldn't even speak to me in English in those days except for a few choice words.

It was necessary to make one trip to Bomet in order to practice our language skills. This should be fun, we thought. Well, at least it will be a challenge. We walk to Bomet because it is only five miles away and we need the exercise. It is a sunny day and this provides a break from Swahili classes.

Kay and I and our friend Denise walk together. We kind of look like the missionary version of the Oreo cookie with Denise being the white icing. Upon our arrival in Bomet, we set about our task conversing with the locals and buying things in the store to practice our Swahili. We have to get the storekeeper to understand that we want new matches not a blue mattress. We do manage to buy some things need in the average African American home, such as a hoe, a pick axe, some chicken feed and some spaghetti. We know how to make our own sauce.

It is time to go home now, but it begins to rain. So what do we do now? We decide we will ride the local matatu bus (read Matatu Hell for more understanding of this). We know how these matatus move. We are aware that many of these vehicles have no brakes.

This really doesn't matter because it can't go too fast because the ruts in the road are too big and a sudden stop can always be managed by hitting a cow or running into one of the rocks on the side of the road.

The only real problem is there is only room for one more person in the front cab. There are three of us. The turnboy (conductor) looks at this Oreo cookie. He has a real problem now. How does he take these foreigners and treat them appropriately? The solution? Segregate us!

There are three persons in the front cab, including the driver, but one more person can be held in place if the rope is tightened on the passenger door handle and the driver leans the right half of his body outside of the car. Now, who rides up front? Well, our friend Denise is white, like the icing on the cookie! This is a no brainer in the conductor's eyes.

Denise is invited up front and Kay and I are directed to the back of the matatu. We are fortunate that we are given the places beneath the tarpaulin instead of hanging on the outside. They do want to treat us a bit better since we are obviously foreigners. I can't believe it! This has never happened to me at home. I come all the way to the 'mother land' to be treated like the second class citizen. Fortunately, Denise has more of Christ in her than to be segregated like this so she sits in the back with us.

Worship services at Tenwek reflect this same attitude. I won't even speculate who is at fault. There is obviously a precedent set here and I am not sure if even Rosa Parks could stop it as she did at in Birmingham Alabama in 1955 by refusing to give her seat to a white person. On any Sunday morning you could have seen the continuation of this segregation. Kenyans who arrived at 10:20 for the 10:30 worship service almost exclusively took seats in the back of the meeting room. Missionaries who arrived at 10:25 for the same service would sit anywhere they wanted, but most frequently in the front and middle sections.

I have been told by my Kenyan friends that since the missionaries were the first elders of the church it was a natural assumption for them to have the front seats. Now, most if not all missionaries are assumed to be preachers, at least in rural settings and still offered the best seats.

I observed this for all of the years I was at Tenwek. I asked the Kenyan men in our Men's Bible Study about this one day. "Why do you guys sit in the back?" I ask. "Even when you come early, you sit in the back" I go on to say. "What is the purpose of this? "

They laugh at me in an uncomfortable way, covering their mouths and snickering. It is not an easy question to answer. No one readily volunteers. I look to a doctor friend of mine in the meeting and he looks away shyly. His face can't turn red.

I remember these are the some of the same guys who told me that 'they were born to pick the white man's tea' on the tea plantations.

"What if" I went on "the missionaries came to the meeting room first and sat in the back? Where would you sit then?"

A strained silence comes over the room. No one had ever thought of this before. This could present a real problem. Then my doctor friend speaks up boldly, with a chuckle; "I guess we'd have to sit outside!"

Carter G. Woodson, the father of Black History in America and the author of The Miseducation of the American Negro has said that 'if you teach a man to use the back door long enough, when he comes to a place that has no back door, he will make a back door.' I was seeing the back door mentality. Someone had obviously set this precedent either intentionally or by neglect. There is no question that this hampered growth in Christ. Somehow the possibility of being an equal person in the eyes of God has never been adequately and effectively transmitted or captured.

Many Kenyans have seized the Gospel as it has been given to them, without fully considering the implications of their accepting all of the trappings it holds. I would venture to say that most white missionaries are completely unaware of these trappings which come with being from a culture which is perceived by many around the world as generally, both arrogant and aggressive.

Again this is no fault of their own. When you grow up in America as a white person, you are most likely to think of yourself and your kind as superior. It is part of the system.

We actually believe that "Little House on the Prairie" is as an accurate depiction of American life as "Roots". Most of the world knows about Roots, but few watch Little House. They know how American encouraged the back door mentality.

We need to help release people from the back door mentality. We need to help people be free to think. We cannot give them the freedom to think. When we give them this freedom, it is not theirs. We must remove our culture from our Christianity. We must do like Moses and claim that God has sent us to "Let my people go....or to re-phrase Let my people think"

I am always amazed at the numbers of Johns, Josephs, Ezekiels and Elijahs in Kenya. It seemed the names of the Bible are so much more common there than here in the US. I asked men from our Bible study why this was so. 'Why do Kenyan men have such names and the women as well, Sara and Zipporah and Leah? Why are these names so common' I ask?

Their response is 'It is the 'Christian name'. They get it when they are baptized.' They were forced early on in missionary conversions, to relinquish their traditional names if they wanted to be accepted in mission schools or for work on mission compounds, or even to be baptized.

'Well, brother Thomas' I go on to ask, 'Why is it always a name like those in the Bible? Why can't you use your Kenyan names as Christian names?'

Amongst the people we work with, people are named in a variety of ways. The male child will take the father's last name as his first name and then will have another name indicating the time or situation at the time of birth. Others have names from their father or mother and then in order of succession in birth, are named for grand parents and great grandparents. There is rhyme and reason to this.

When the name is for situation or time of birth, it may be recorded as; when the cows come home, or time of getting water, or an important guest has arrived. Such names have meaning and significance to the family. But now it appears one must have a Christian name. I am told that the name must be a Biblical name, which I know doesn't mean much because Beelzebub and Jezebel are in the Bible and no one names their child such.

Also, I have met many a Stanley and Cynthia, names I have not read in the Bible. But it appears that a western name is equivalent with a Christian name and an African name cannot be so. We have encouraged people to disassociate from their names of their ancestry, advising them that such names are completely devoid of Christianity and to take names associated with the west which automatically are Christian.

If people can think, they can see themselves as a reflection of Christ and not a reflection of the missionary who taught them about Christ. This will allow our Kenyan brothers to sit anywhere they want in the church building and worship and fear God and not the people who taught them about God.

MATATU HELL

If you've never been to a developing or non-industrialized nation, you can't

get this picture very well. But try it anyway. A matatu (pronounced mu as in mud, ta as in tot, tu as in too) is any vehicle designed to carry a limited load of people or things which exceeds that limit by a multiple of three to four. In other words, take your typical small minivan designed for 6-8 passengers in the US and put 18 to 20 people in it. Now, load the top of the van with their belongings, baskets and boxes of clothes, crates of live chickens, a bicycle and maybe someone's new piece of furniture. Load both the front and back fenders and bumpers with softer items, large fish, small mattresses and light weight buckets. You have just created a matatu.

The joke goes, 'how many people can you fit into a matatu? The answer is; 'one more!'

This vehicle is often times nothing more than a 'bucket of mismatched nuts and bolts' held together with rust. The fenders and body are beaten and misshapen by several accidents. The doors are fitted with a variety of devices serving as handles, often times rope or knobs from other makes and models.

The passengers inside are in a variety of positions, some sitting, some standing, and some crouching. Many of them are forced to place their less ceremonious body parts in the faces of their fellow travelers or out of the open windows when it is not raining too hard.

The conductor or 'turn-boy' serves to squeeze people into and off of the vehicle at its frequent stops and to collect the fares. This person must keep an eye out for competing vehicles and waiting passengers as well as holding on to his own place for dear life, in the vehicle on the many curves and bumps.

Now to make this trip 'breathtaking', many of these people have been traveling for many hours sometimes days without the benefit of water or other essentials of personal body hygiene. They are tired and hungry. They are poor and travel this way because, there is no other way.

This van has not been inspected by anyone since it was pressed into service. The only times the brakes are checked is when moving at an uncontrollable speed and slowing down is necessary to avoid running over the policeman waiting for a chance to inspect the vehicle, or even get a little 'monetary compensation' at the bottom of the hill. This is considered bad form, because the policemen are reportedly an essential part of the unrecognized underground economy.

The passengers who cannot fit in the van hold on to the outside railing, or on the open doors of the van. They get the added benefit of the wind in their face and the rain over their bodies. This comes at no change of rider fees and if they hit a bump and are lost on the road with an open skull fracture, there is no refund.

These kind of vehicles and their bigger counterparts the buses are commonly on the roads of Kenya and also found in what Kay and I have called, Matatu Hell.

Matatu Hell is a bus station. There is a Matatu Hell in most of the major towns of Kenya and all of the cities. These places look the same. Dozens of dilapidated vehicles, spewing diesel fumes as they race their motors, honking their horns incessantly and yelling for passengers to board as they compete for fares. Crowds of people are in these places, carrying their loads on their backs, heads arms. Men, women, boys and girls are climbing aboard and praying that they will reach their destination alive with all their body parts and belongings.

The fatality rates on these roads are incredible were literally in the thousand deaths yearly according to a newsletter published by the Kenyatta National Hospital in August 1999. This is in a nation with fewer vehicles than any one small city in America. These statistics are borne out in an article published in the East and Central Africa Journal of Surgery in December 1999. The article quoted mortality and morbidity rates from road traffic accidents in 1985, comparing such nations as Britain, Canada, Japan, Nigeria and Kenya. In Britain, for instance, there were 6 deaths and 311 injuries for every 10,000 vehicles on the road. In Kenya, there were 55 deaths and 500 injuries for every 10,000 vehicles and Nigeria 125 deaths and 1,750 injuries for every 10,000 vehicles.

During the month of April of 2000, there were two major accidents involving buses, in which the immediate death toll exceeded 140 persons, not counting those who survived to be admitted to hospitals and later succumbed to their injuries. People allow themselves to be degraded to a state lower than animals in order to gamble their very lives and limbs, hoping they will arrive at a given destination at some point in time.

"Kai square!' This means move over as close as you can to the next person, making your 'buttocks and body as close to a square as possible. This is a familiar term to anyone who has sat on a matatu, especially as a young man, may be forced to sit across from an elderly woman, with his knees in between hers. It is not within the culture to offend the elderly in this way, but remember again, this is hell.

If the bus or van or small car breaks down on the desolate roads of Kenya, there is no one to service it, except the over-worked driver with the marijuana like buzz and his oft times inebriated assistant. They may or may not have a spare tire and it may or may not have air or treads. A breakdown on the road is bad because it subjects the passengers to winds of fate. Robbers and thieves are on the roads.

If you do break down or have an accident, your belongings are sometimes shared with strangers who pick your pockets and bags and luggage. There are no accommodations. There may be no food. There are no restrooms with functioning toilets. The only things that separate Matatu Hell from eternal Hell is that you pay for this experience in Kenya shillings and people pray harder to get out of Matatu Hell.

As I consider these places and these people, I am reminded of the tremendous burden the average Kenyan faces just to carry out the ordinary things in life. I will only know such struggles from a distance, I pray. This is a way of life. Most Kenyans can't get here from there in Kenya without passing through hell.

As of the printing of this book, much has changed about Matatu hell. Bribes are fewer, so they say, passengers are treated with more respect and there is a speed and load limit imposed on all vehicles. The death rates have been cut by at least 70% by instituting some of these measures. In this instance, hell has changed.

DIS BE AFRICA

It is commonly said that we have to adjust to late arrivals, late departures, empty shelves and empty rhetoric because 'This is Africa." The eponym for this is "TIA".

Now for those of you who know anything about Ebonics (a much maligned black American dialect), you recognize that the word 'is' can be substituted by 'be'. So you do not have 'This is Africa' but 'This be Africa.' Well, from there it is only a matter of losing a bit of the diction your mother used to tell you and you have 'Dis be Africa' or DBA. I know I will get into a lot of trouble for that one. Anyway, we do this in many ways other than just linguistics.

Now I know such things exist in other parts of the world. I know that the former Soviet Union and its satellites are known for shortages. But I don't work there, so allow me some leeway to explain how things work, or don't work where I am.

Consider our experiences in Kenya for instance. As I said, we are used to having late arrivals and empty shelves. DBA. It is not unusual to go into a restaurant, order your food and wait for thirty or forty minutes just to be told that 'We just discovered we do not have that today.' It is not unusual to go into the post office to purchase stamps to be told, 'We have run out of the 15 Shilling stamp', or when you ask for a receipt to be asked 'Did you bring a piece of paper for that?'

People have had their homes burglarized or cars stolen and upon calling the police to come to investigate are informed 'We will come to the scene of the crime if you will come get us, as we have no car, or no gas for the car' . The fire department is known for arriving at some scenes to ask 'where is the water?' I could go on and on..., but you get the picture don't you? DBA!

We had purchased our new Volkswagen van out of a catalog. It was impossible to do otherwise from where we were. The auto dealer in Kericho was a three-hour drive from Tenwek at that time as there was no paved road for half of the trip. So we made the weekly grocery trip to town for the mission station and stopped by the dealer to pick our car out of the picture book. No, he did not have a parking lot full of shiny new cars in the back. He just had this picture book. DBA!

He brought us the car several weeks later, for a test drive. He arrived at Tenwek with the driver. Many people use drivers in Kenya. We invited them in for lunch. He said he could join us, but the driver couldn't. As I said, many people USE drivers in Kenya. Two black Kenyans, however, they are considered of different classes and hence the driver had to stay outside and eat. DBA.

We test-drove our new van. A stripped down VW van with the only accessories being windshield wipers and hubcaps. $25,000. No radio! How is a black man gonna drive a car without a radio?! We were desperate. We needed someway to get out of the middle of nowhere if it was just to drive to nowhere else. We had spent several months at Tenwek unable to get away out of the unseasonable mud from the heavier than normal rains. We were willing to buy donkeys if necessary. We bought the van. We decided we could sing if we needed music.

After several weeks the inside panel on the sliding door came off of the frame. We tried everything, glue, tape, paste, and screws to keep it in place but nothing worked. We wrote the dealer to inform him of our problem. He told us to bring the car to the dealership in Kisumu, (only four hours away at that time) to fix it. We complied.

You can imagine what happened or have you not been paying attention? DBA. Of course they didn't have the part! Are you surprised?

Not to worry Dr. Johnson. We can have that part very soon' the man says to me in a very affable way. I am pleased with his calm reassurance and I am sure he will not disappoint me.

Maybe I'm not paying attention. DBA

After two more trips to the dealers showroom, we figure it out. We write the board members of the corporation in London. Within one month, the dealer is at our doorstep with the part. 'The driver is outside right now, ready to put the part on' he explains as though out of breath.

"Thank you so much" I reply.

He goes on 'please don't write the board again like that Dr. Johnson. It causes a lot of trouble. We are very sorry it took so long to get you the part.'

I feel sorry for the guy and I am determined to improve our relationship. We decide we will allow the garage people at his dealership to service our car on its scheduled maintenance. We need an oil change and the brakes are in need of replacement.

So we make the four-hour drive to Kisumu with some friends who are visiting us from the US.

'Dr. Johnson, we are so glad to see you again' the young man at the counter says excitedly! 'We were so sorry to disappoint you. We won't allow that to happen again!'

'It is okay', I reply calmly. 'I came in early today in order to get you to change my oil and fix the brakes. Do you have any idea of how long that will take?'

Dr. Johnson, because it is you and you are here so early, we can make this a very fast job. We should be able to do this in less than four hours and have it ready no later than 12:00 noon' he says, with his whole face smiling and eager.

It wont be necessary for noon I say, we will eat lunch at noon, but 2:00 would be nice. We plan to go shopping with our friends and then we will come back at 2:00. What do you think?'

'That is good Dr. Johnson. But I assure you we will be finished by noon!'

'Okay, then I will be here at 1:00 just after lunch' I say and we leave the garage and go into town.

Kay and I and our guests wander around the town and find there is not as much to do as we had anticipated. Lunch is a bit under whelming, but filling so we make it back to the garage.

'Oh hi Dr. Johnson' the man says a lot less eagerly!

Detecting the hesitation in his voice I ask 'Well, is the car ready?'

'Uuuuhhh, we have changed the oil and we are working on the brakes' he says with a timid smile.

'That's good. How long will the brake job take?'

'We don't have any brake pads.'

'What do you mean?' I start to sweat a little.

We took your old pads off and we looked in our shop and could not find any pads to replace yours.'

'So what do you plan to do?' I ask as I feel my mouth go dry.

He smiles and says 'We are going to order some brake pads right now!'

'That's good!' I say, somewhat relieved. 'How long will it take to finish the work then?'

'Well, we have to send to Nairobi for the pads. That will take at least two days'

Now I feel my pulse quicken. 'Do you mean I am supposed to wait here for you to get those brakes from Nairobi?'

Kay has been quiet all of this time. She moves in quickly as she sees the beads of sweat on my forehead. I feel her restrain me from climbing over the counter.

I offer the ultimate American threat 'Let me see your supervisor!'

He disappears and out comes a guy wearing a tie and carrying a clipboard. 'Can I help you?' Kay goes on to explain things. At this point as she is afraid that I will break the man's clipboard.

'We are told that you don't have brake pads' she says sweetly.

'That is right miss. But we can order you some from Nairobi.'

She goes on to explain, 'We don't have time for this, and we must be back to work tomorrow morning at Tenwek Hospital.'

Well, we do have some refurbished brake pads we could put on your car' he offers apologetically.

'Are these refurbished pads any better than those on the car now?' I see the sweat on her forehead now.

'No, the refurbished pads are no better' he admits.

'Can you tell me why I would buy brake pads that are as bad as those I already have? Does that make sense to you?' I look at her closely because I think she is going to grab the man's tie.

'I'll put your old ones back on, but it will have to wait until after lunch'

We leave the dealer at 3:00, right on time. DBA.

KICKING THE CASKET

Most funerals are sad events to me. This one kind of made me afraid. It was kinda like Little Big Horn and Custer's last stand. I really thought I had started a major international event. It was a funeral of a local influential person. He was of the predominant tribe in the region we were visiting. I happened to look like I was not from that tribe, which did not bode well in this era of multi-party politics. Multi-party politics is something we take for granted, though it has not been long in existence in the US either.

When our nation was founded, the only party was those of white men with money. White men who did not own land, women and anyone of color could not vote. World Book Encyclopedia notes that until the 19th amendment to the US Constitution in 1920, women could not vote. Native Americans could not participate in elections until 1948 and citizens of Washington DC (of whom a great percentage were of African descent) had to wait until the 23rd amendment to the Constitution to gain the right to vote in Presidential elections in 1961.

It was not until 1970 that the US Supreme Court outlawed the many tests black Americans were required to pass in order to exercise their right to vote. Black people were killed in great numbers for this right to vote. Lynchings, public beatings and disappearances of prominent and common people were normal commonplace occurrences in the US during until the latter part of 20th century. Political involvement for African Americans could mean death.

According to "African Americans and the American Political System" by Lucius J. Barker and Mack H. Jones, the registration of black people climbed from 60 to 64 percent from 1966-1988, closing a previous percentage gap between whites of 10 points to three points. Black people voted their voice the loudest in the 1992 election of President Bill Clinton who received just 39 percent of the white vote. Black and white voters and opinions remain widely disparate today.

Multiparty politics in America is new at best. Our family has watched it unfold in Kenya. We were part of the political landscape because any large institution has political pull. We went to many events and occasions because to avoid them often spoke of your political leaning. This could be dangerous for your institution as we continued to learn.

At the coercion of the United States which knew a lot about human rights having denied its citizens such for almost three centuries, and all the other big players of the international politics, Kenya finally introduced multi-party politics in 1992. I found it so strange how our American ambassador demanded multi-party politics for a nation whose independence was still new at 25 years, when the US was still learning about including all of its citizens in the political process. We were demanding full representative democracy in 25 years when we had only come close after more than 200 years.

Racial wars were common in 19th and 20th century America and we were lecturing people on how to overcome the differences of centuries. However, because foreign aid was withheld and the leaders were convinced that development could not proceed without it, Kenya acquiesced.

With the onset of multiparty politics, Kenya's tribal clashes became even more violent and literally hundreds of people were being killed. We could sit in our living room at Tenwek some days and see men walking out of the surrounding forests, carrying spears and arrows going to hunt down the enemy within.

They would burn whole communities, kill men, women and children, just to drive these foreign tribes, these troublemakers out of their land. These events still occur with the most recent wholesale killings in the resort town of Mombasa where hundreds of 'out of towners' were butchered in the streets in 1996 and 1997.

As events unfolded before us in Bomet in 1992, one of the hospital board members was killed in the not so distant hills. He was a very prominent and respected elder statesmen. The family never found his heart as it was removed from his body by the raiders as they burned his field of crops and his house. I was told by some Kenyans that organ removal is done to keep the family of the deceased unsettled. There is some mystical and spiritual symbolism of burying a body with portions missing.

I attended to many of these casualties of war in the hospital. Those who made it were often wounded by pangas (machetes) and arrows. If the arrows were 'nuclear tipped' (as they would refer to the poison tips), the victim would die in the field. Soldiers and police were unable to stop the fighting and this continued for months and even smolders now.

So, here I am in Kenya at this funeral. They had no problem with multi-party politics, as long as there was only 'one multi-party.' I did not look like one of them, so everything I could be suspect.

This was not a funeral of one a victim of tribal clashes. This was the funeral of the brother of an important person in this community. I did not look like these people, even though we as black people in America think we all look alike. Or is that some other people who say that? It was like being a black Jew in a Neo-Nazi rally. As I said before out of tribe strangers in these parts of the country, had been known to have a donate their organs, while still in use, without signing the donor card.

We were filing past the casket. It was situated on the side of a hill, seated on two chairs. The grass beneath the casket was moist from the recent rains. There were hundreds of neighbors and friends, family and curious people at this event. This was an important person who died. It was no laughing matter, at least not until I arrived.

People were standing in the rain looking down at Kay and me as we filed past the casket. They had their umbrellas shielding them from this soft rain under a cloudy sky. They were not happy people. They were about to be less happy. I looked in that little window on the casket and saw the deceased, dressed neatly in black. Sure looked dead to me!

The line behind me was long with mourners who wanted to pay their respects to the dead man. The people on the hill had yet to make it down to see the body, but because Doctor Johnson was there, the visiting 'pretend to be white man', who happened to look like one of the enemy tribes, I was given deference to view the body at my leisure and kinda first in line.

As I walked by the casket having saluted the dead and saying a brief prayer in my heart, I turned my attention to the people at the head end of the casket, grieving family members who warmly shook my hand thanking me for taking the time out of my busy day to show respect to their beloved. That's when I heard it. Kerplunk! Or was it a bang? Well it was some kinda thud or noise!

All I know is that as I looked behind me, the casket was on the ground, face down. Luckily the body didn't fall out.

The people on the hill began to wail and cry. I really felt like the nigger-kike surrounded by swastikas and hooded riders. I broke into a bit of a sweat. I knew there was no way to escape. Only an angel of mercy could get me out of this. Well the angel appeared. He stood and calmed the crowd. That angel assured the crowd that this ignorant American, black white man was not a member of the enemy tribe, just a clumsy oaf who meant well.

We were invited for the reception, but Kay said she was afraid I would tip over the food tray, so we left. I tell the truth here, I did not kick that casket, no matter what she will tell you in her version of the story.

IS ANYONE SAFE AROUND HERE? OR THE KIPSIGIS VERSION OF "THE OUT OF TOWNERS"

I sit here watching a movie about white lynch mobs in America. All good Bible believing white folks. Confederate flag waving, cross burning, sheet wearing gun toting, conservative white folk, chasing down black folks like hunting deer and killing roaches. They do it in God's name. Saving America for the good Christian white folks. Saving America from the boogey man, the nigger.

It was a dark night. I hate stories that start with that kind of sentence. But, it was a dark night.

Well how about this for a start? What is worse than a white mob searching for a black man on a dark road in rural America? I'll tell you. A black mob searching for another black man in rural Africa, especially when they can't distinguish you from the people for whom they search. That is right. Lynching in Kenya is as commonplace today as barbecues and cookouts in America. In fact, fire and burning flesh is an important part of this tradition too.

I remember seeing it in pictures in America, with black men hanging from trees or on bonfires for somehow insulting the white race. These pictures scared me from ever wanting to go into any part of white America as I thought their version of burning flesh on an open pit was not the kind of holiday I could enjoy. So here I am in Africa, safe from lynch mobs!

Fortunately for Kay and me, white missionaries were amongst us this dark night. There have been a few occasions we have been warned not to leave the compound unless we were accompanied by a white missionary. As I said before and will say again, it is good to be with white people in Africa, sometimes.

It was rather eerie. We heard the yells and screams of a dozen or so KIPSIGIS men hiding in trees. They had already made at least one assault on the hospital compound. They were intent on murdering the Ogutas, a family of four. The mother, Domatilla, was a nurse on the hospital surgical wards and the husband, John, worked in accounting with Kay. The two children were hiding with the mother in one room and the father and a friend were trying to hold the front door as men with axes and machetes tried to break it down.

Domatilla looked out the keyhole and saw John struggling to save their lives. She heard the anger of the lynch mob. She heard their cursing and drunken oaths recited in the darkness of that night. She heard the splintering of the door and felt a sure doom. She could in her mind no doubt see the bodies of her family with blood splattered around the house. But then Domatilla says she opened her eyes even wider. She saw the Hand of God reach out and hold back the door, just as the crowd outside heard her yelling; "Jesus, Jesus, Jesus." Their response was, "its only women and children, let's leave them alone."

We missionary men ran to the scene after being alerted of the danger by one of the staff at the hospital. We were in a missionary station meeting. We were praying about the tribal conflict brewing on the compound and how it was necessary for us to carry out our assigned duties in orderly missionary like fashion. Little did we know that at that very moment, the lives of men and women were being threatened. The call came over the mission compound phones. We rushed to the scene. We arrived just in time to see the men regrouping for a renewed attack on the Oguta home.

We ran the quarter mile up to the hospital compound entrance way. We placed ourselves between the gateway leading to the house and the group of men who were yelping like animals and screaming from high up in trees and behind bushes along the road. We stood there, led by Dr. Ernie Steury. Dr Steury was the first physician to come to Tenwek hospital full time and for the first ten years the only physician.

Dr. Steury had over the past 25 plus years served as obstetrician, pediatrician, pastor, medical doctor, hospital administrator, hospital executive officer counselor for the church, preacher, teacher, undertaker, mortician and on many occasions burial crew. Many people amongst the Kipsigis refused to bury their own dead. They didn't mind this white man doing it. Except for Clark Kent, Ernie Steury is the only Superwhiteman I have ever known.

Dr. Steury had been in the Tenwek community for a long time. Everyone knows Dr. Steury. Everyone respects Dr. Steury. Everyone except the man wielding the machete in Dr. Steury's face. He and about eight or ten other men stood there in the middle of the night waving their weapons at us and most threateningly at Dr. Steury. We were all scared. I was very scared because at least they were white. Killing a white man is still frowned upon in Kenya.

White people seem to have such a great deal of protection. Not only because

they are white of course, but because they represent a power from beyond the shores which can actually change the balance of power in a given region of the country. Historically in Kenya, you don't kill a white man unless you want trouble. I am told that historically, you don't even argue or fight a white man even if you were in the right as a black Kenyan. You could be arrested just for not submitting to his will.

For the past several years since our arrival in Kenya, the news headlines have been filled with the Julie Ward murder. This story is of a young British woman who was killed while camping in a game reserve. There have been numerous investigations by the feared Kenya CID (Criminal Investigation Division) and even Scotland Yard. There have been Kenyan police, politicians and game reserve guards investigated, probed, questioned, harassed, accused and even sometimes jailed with little resolution over the exact circumstances of Julie Ward's death.

In the same time, hundreds of Kenyan school children have died in bus accidents, drownings, epidemics and disasters. I can't name one of these young black Kenyan lives. However, the name of Julie Ward has to quote American rap artist Kool Moe Dee left a "stain on the brain" of Kenyans.

This kind of stain reminds them that their lives are of little notice when compared to a white person. Don't kill a white man in Kenya. You will be in trouble.

It is pretty much the same in America of course. Black people don't kill white people because justice is not color blind. Now killing a black missionary would be a mistake to be sure, but by the time they discovered you were only a black man pretending to be white, it would be too late and "oooppss!" does not look good on a headstone. It would be easy to kill a black man like me and get away with it.

Just like those white conservatives in America got away with it in "the good old days." Killing a white missionary would get Kenyans in trouble. But for me it meant I am in trouble. I am as in much trouble as the Ogutas. I found it even more dangerous as time went on.

We must have been surrounded by angels. Dr. Steury slowly talked to the men and convinced them that killing was not in the best interest of the hospital or the community. The man raised his machete and swung it in Dr. Steury's face and stated "Just because you are a white man doesn't mean you won't bleed." He lowered the knife and bit his own arm and started to cry. He could not bring himself to cut this white man. The man convinced his co-conspirators to cease and desist.

That night we missionary men secretly moved the family and several other members of the staff who had been threatened to a safer location in the hospital. There is a portion of the hospital where the money is kept. There are steel bars and cement walls. We moved the staff here under the cover of dark.

We had tried calling the Bomet police. We told them we were in danger of being overrun by the community thugs and schoolboys who wanted every out of tribe member of the staff put out at once. The police informed us that they could not get through the roads as the roads were blocked by the schoolboys and they did not have a police car. They, however would come to our aid if we could pick them up in one of our cars.

It was obvious the Calvary could not help us. I would have even welcomed John Wayne. We were on our own. We stayed in the office with the staff for a long time and as the night became colder and darker, we became more scared. Some of us men took shifts and stayed with them for several hours. We didn't know if and when the attackers would breech the walls of the compound. We were afraid for their lives and ours.

The night passed. No one was injured except the young painter who had been taken by force from his home and marched around the compound with a knife to his throat. He was told he must give the names of any people of his tribe and their location or be killed. They made a small laceration to his cheek to show they were serious. They let him go and he later joined us in the safe place with the others in hiding. We didn't know what to do from there. Dr. Steury bade all the missionaries go home and rest. We did and he went on to make arrangements for a plane to come and fly the endangered staff out of Tenwek the next morning. It was a long night. We survived.

The next morning the front of the hospital was filled with angry community members. They were not angry at the perpetrators or instigators. They were angry that the hospital had harbored these evil elements of non-Kipsigis tribe members. Literally hundreds of people lined the roads, crowded the hospital entrance and hung around waiting for something to happen. We looked for who was going to make it happen.

They were mad at all of us for hiding the out of towners. We put ourselves around these out of towners like a human shield as they loaded themselves in the car and made their way to the airstrip in Bomet about five miles away. As the caravan of cars carrying missionaries and this family of four, the painter and our Swahili teacher made its way out of the compound, I was reminded of all the fears I felt being chased by angry white mobs in Chicago, just for crossing the tracks, or sitting on their part of the beach.

There were at least two other occasions when I felt this fear while in Kenya. I have yet to understand the deep and bitter hate which drives people to kill because of a difference in tribe and custom. I have heard Kenyan church leaders justify the hate and prejudice they feel for one another. I have come to understand that the most dangerous thing one can do in this situation is to open one's mouth in defense of someone. There is no one safe in this situation and we were only kept by God's grace.

DIVORCE? NEVER!
BUT SHE'D LIKE TO KILL HIM!

As we in America wrestle with our personal civil rights and whether or not the tribulation is here or coming next year before Wal-Mart is bought up by Micro-Soft, people in the poorer parts of the world are wrestling with less mundane issues of life. We find it amazing that as we doubly filter our water and worry about static cling, most people in Kenya are trying to decide if they have enough energy to live another day.

Is life worth the hassle of spending 80% of the time looking for clean water and dry wood? Some mothers in Kenya have decided it is not worth it and have thrown their children in wells to drown..., and then dove in behind them as recorded in one recent Kenyan newspaper.

Being a wife in Kenya takes a lot of energy. Being a mother takes a lot of courage. Not being a mother when married is impossible because it can cost you your life. A woman must face choices between death and death. If she doesn't bear a child, she may be relegated to the position of the second wife, or worse yet, chased away Almost as importantly she must bear a male child to be a good wife. (No one reminds the men that it is they who bear the 'Y' chromosome which determines male gender as the woman holds only the 'X'.) If she does get pregnant, she has a 2-5% chance of dying before she delivers her baby or shortly afterwards. Divorce is not an option.

As I discuss our extremely high divorce rates in America with my Kenyan counterparts, I am embarrassed. They are amazed at how easily our homes break up in America. "Do you mean a woman can leave her husband if he does not treat her right? What kind of marriages do you have there?"

At first I am really disturbed. Maybe they are right. Then a closer look tells me, many of these Kenyan wives would like divorce, but they don't have that option. I have taken care of husbands who have been poisoned by their wives.

Many men have come to me convinced that the tumors they have or the diseases they have are caused by some spell cast upon them by their distraught wives.

First wives, second wives and even third wives have been known to send their oldest sons as 'hit-men' to take father out at all costs. These men come to the hospital with panga (machete) wounds, human bites and arrows in a variety of places. They want me to help counsel their errant wife, or wives.

Many of these women have been tried in the fire because of the conditions of their lifestyles. One tribe of Kenyans practices courtship by having the couple wrestle. The man and woman compete in hand-to-hand combat. If the woman wins, the man is considered unworthy of her hand. This is so because this particular people live in a desolate wilderness and if the male spouse cannot defeat his wife, it is thought unlikely that he can defend her.

Once a Kenyan woman is married, at least in our part of the country, she ceases to be a part of her own family. The husband has paid a dowry of cows or other livestock. Sometimes money or property is exchanged. This is traditionally out of respect for what the family has invested in this young bride. If she has been to school and learned a trade or profession, the dowry is even of greater value. This tradition can obviously be corrupted.

The government of Kenya is wrestling with the corruption of this system as some families sell their young daughters to old men. Families desperate for money have been known to give their young daughters (as young as 12 years) in marriage.

Even in the best of circumstances, the woman has no real say in most homes in Kenya. She is 'one of the children' of the husband. If you happen to visit some homes in rural Kenya and the wife is home alone, she may not answer at all. In fact, if you ask if anyone is there, she may answer, 'no one is here'.

Kay and I had the opportunity to be invited to a home for lunch in rural Kenya by one of the hospital workers. He happened to be called to work upon our arrival. The wife was not the least bit disturbed by his absence, and had prepared a very delicious meal for us, including our children. She served us in the dining area and promptly went and stayed in the kitchen the entire duration of our visit. She neither conversed with us, nor acknowledge our presence, other than to see to it that our second and third portions were adequate and that the tea was sweet. She bid us farewell as we left, and 'that was that!'

A husband can do what he wants with this wife in many communities and clans as long as he does not kill her. It is only then that he may suffer the consequences of the law. He is the law in his home. If she does not abide by his law, is childless, or does not service him well, she can be dismissed.

One such instance came to my attention in the hospital. The wife was pregnant by her husband. The child was due in three months. The husband decided he no longer wanted her as he had found another wife. He is still by law and tradition allowed to have many wives. Each of the new wives is still subject to his rule and law. In this situation she no longer satisfied him as she relates the story. He sent her to her parents.

Of course she no longer belongs to her parents. The parents, however, agree to take her in only if she will get rid of the baby. Abortion is illegal. She decides she will seek an illegal abortion. Someone performs it. She almost dies as a consequence.

She is admitted to the hospital several days later in toxic shock, confused, anemic, bleeding and near death. I perform an emergency hysterectomy and she lives. She recovers after a long hospitalization and I have the opportunity to introduce her to Jesus. She is anxious to know of the Savior who will accept her. Everyone else has rejected her. This is indeed a memorable occasion for both of us.

I don't know what became of her when she left the hospital. I do hope and pray she was able to get herself out of this marriage. Do I advocate divorce? No! Do I advocate murder? Certainly not! I do pray that God provides her and the other hundreds of thousands of Kenyan wives safe haven because they have so few alternatives. They have no property, no education and no rights. They don't worry about static cling as the typical American wife. They want to know "Is life worth living?"

BOTTLES TO HEAVEN OR HELL

There are certain things you don't argue about. One of those things is refunding your coke bottles to the local retailer. You cannot win this argument. It would be easier to argue with the Hindu that at least one of the one hundred million gods of their faith is not real. You bought the soda, you bought the bottle. Once you have the bottle, the only way to give it back is to get another soda. You cannot return the bottle otherwise.

The bottle lip must not have any chips or cracks, otherwise, you cannot use it even to get a new soda. So the local retailer, which is often some guy on the roadside under a tree with a stack of coke cases filled with soda, inspects every single bottle. He is determined not to let you get any of those bottles past him and his keen eyes. He is equally determined that you will help relieve him of his inventory of sodas. He's gonna win. You want the sodas and all you have is empty bottles.

To this date, there are no doubt missionaries who have long died after having served in Kenya who have bottles in storage awaiting their resurrection to glory and a refund on their coke bottles. Of course in hell a cold coke won't help and certainly an empty bottle would only be more torture.

Upon our return to the US in 1998, we had to give our bottles to friends in Kenya, kind of in escrow, to redeem as they bought more sodas. Things run like this in Kenya. There are traditions which defy any reason. There are things which are done, even though we know it is detrimental to the nation, but tradition does serve a purpose after all...,tradition!

For instance, amongst the Kipsigis people whom we have served we rarely see any of the beasts of burden, like the donkeys, pulling carts. I have never seen a human being on the back of any animal in that region of the country. I have been told it is because it would be unfair to the animal. Others have told me it is undignified to be seen on the beast.

I think there must be some precedent in the Bible of someone important riding on a donkey on at least one occasion. And of course it is much more expedient to allow people to carry their burdens on their heads than to make a cart pulled by animals.

There are other ramifications for being stuck in tradition, much more dangerous than keeping the wheel a secret. Ask people of the Luo tribe of the tradition of the brother inheriting the wife of the other brother who died from AIDS. Tradition dictates that before his brother can be buried, he must sleep with the wife. As we look at the Luo tribe, we see a tribe being decimated by the AIDS epidemic where most of the deaths in the region are no longer attributable to malaria, cholera, typhoid, meningitis and dehydration and starvation.

As late as June 13 2004, an article in the *Daily Nation* quotes one scholar's view on wife inheritance. Professor Ochola Ayayo states that the widow must be 'accompanied' as she needs a partner after the death of her husband. It is a long held tradition and in Professor Ayayo's, opinion; "...*if her husband has died of HIV/ AIDS and if by bad luck the person re-marrying her is not infected, then I think society should not mind one person being sacrificed as opposed to hundreds of others. The logic here is simple-to have the 'dangerous woman' confined*"

Professor Ayayo continues his description of these traditions, by defining the term 'joter'. His is a 'strange breed of men of low social standing' who are paid to marry or have sex with widows as part of a cleansing ceremony. He explains this custom as *'...cord cutting..., creating a new link between the dead man and the widow, as custom never allowed a married woman to have sex with another man other than her husband...., owing to poverty, these fellows are now everywhere looking for opportunity to perform the ritual. But if only they can be disciplined, then society can take solace from the fact that this lot with a high HIV/AIDS risk infection mainly thrives on clients who are equally infected....it is not demeaning to a woman, as it is primarily meant to be supportive by driving away her loneliness.'*

Meshack Riaga Ogallo is quoted in the same newspaper of May 12, 2005 is quoted stating; *'...We know that AIDS is spreading fast in the community because of this practice, but we will not discard our culture just because AIDS is here. We cannot have a people without a culture. Wife inheritance is an indispensable culture to our community. We know its benefits and we will stand by it.'*

Whole families as much as 50-60 percent of the populations in certain regions of the country are dying from HIV infection alone. The Kenya Ministry of Health of Kenya has several publications dealing with the AIDS epidemic. These publications include the Strategic Plan for 1999-2004, a position paper "AIDS in Kenya" for 1999 and a Sessional Paper No. 4 of 1997. AIDS rates vary from 10-38% around the nation. The highest prevalence being in the second decade of life for women and the third decade for men.

The government acknowledges in these publications that socio-cultural factors predominate as one of the major causes of the continuing epidemic. With regard to cultural issues, the Sessional Paper states: "Cultural beliefs and practices were useful in maintaining biological continuity, socialization of young people, maintaining law and order, defining the meaning of life...

,also providing the capacity for societies to cope with calamities such as drought and disease outbreaks.

With the advent of AIDS, some of these beliefs and practices require reexamination, because they promote behaviors which put individuals at risk. These include different types of marital union like, polygamy, woman to woman marriage...., widow inheritance...., rites of circumcision, ritual bathing of the dead, ear piercing, scarification and tattooing with contaminated instruments.

"The predominantly patriarchal Kenyan communities prescribe a high status for men which at times involves risk taking... ,male sexual prowess, ego and need to glorify virility. The status of African women within the society is contingent on child bearing with the preference for male off-springs. This affects decisions on family size, fertility and sexuality. Cultural, biological and personal considerations influence early sexuality activity on young girls. Socialization of girls in many communities dictates permissiveness thus creating a situation where girls cannot negotiate or reject sexual advances."

In the Daily Nation article of July 23, 1999 entitled "Moi's prescription for war on Aids" ; the reporter quotes the President of Kenya advocating abstinence from casual sex for two years to help curb the spread of Aids.

Another story from an April 1999 edition of the Daily Nation newspaper in Kenya. History is being made in the anti-Aids campaigns in Nyanza Province in western Kenya, where groups of widows have decided to openly rebel against long held cultural practices which have been blamed for the spread of the scourge.

Last week, 13 Aids widows met US envoy to Kenya Prudence Bushnell in Kisumu and gave her a 30-minute spine-chilling tale of their personal, social and economic problems which are frustrating their efforts to achieve their goal.

The 13, who included a 80-year-old grandmother, said they were caring for 63 Aids orphans yet all have no formal employment, business or any other means of steady income.

The granny narrated how she lost four sons and six in-laws to the killer disease in a space of three years. Most of her colleagues had between two and nine children in their charge, some having dropped out of school for lack of fees. while others cried for better housing.

Asked by the envoy what message they would like to convey to Kenyans about their plight and dreams, one of the widows replied in an emotional voice: "I would like to say that I have accepted that Aids is really here because it claimed my husband, other relatives and friends. I advise the public to keep off irresponsible sex... let us not kill others knowingly.

Says the official: "The death of a husband usually renders the women vulnerable to accepting relatives' demands, including ritual sexual cleansing which is often the most risky. If she completely rejects these practices, the woman may lose ownership or access to some of the family property.

This article only underscores the importance of stopping some traditions and customs. One commonly held myth is that when a man contracts a sexually transmitted disease if he can sleep with a young virgin, he will be cured. Hence, parents will often sell their young daughters in their early teen years for financial gain or food or other favors. These girls go on to become pregnant and infected with a variety of sexually transmitted diseases which they in turn pass on to their offspring.

When talking with one Kenyan physician friend of mine he stated that one big error donor nations make in combating AIDS in Africa was in trying to find the "high risk group." He states that since we in America had found such groups in the drug addicts and homosexuals, we thought we would find such groups in Kenya. The problem of controlling AIDS in Kenya is not the same because everyone in Kenya is potentially in the high-risk group because of tradition and custom.

These same donors promote condoms as opposed to abstinence because they don't want to appear to be moralizing about sex. The condoms come from overseas and are promoted on television and are available in gas stations, general stores, bars and hotels. The problem is, the common man may never visit most of these places on a frequent basis. When he does visit these places, he may or may not find a condom.

If he does find a condom, it most likely has traveled a long way under dubious packing conditions and may have not survived without holes and cracks. The nanometer of space it takes to allow a sperm to traverse one of these holes is a crevice when the thousands of HIV viruses arrive at the same place. Condoms are not the answer in Kenya. Just visit my clinic with me and see the number of veneral warts and herpes rashes from the virsuses shed from the scrotal and labial skin, not covered by condoms and you will be convinced that condoms are not the answer.

The *EastAfrican* Magazine of July 11-17 2005 writes how "Uganda Faces Condom Shortage." In this article, only 20 percent of the required condoms were available from the World Bank funding. I myself wonder why it is impossible to control this urge for sex, while the same men can control their urinary bladders and anal sphincters. Why do anyone consider it rude or unsanitary to defecate or urinate uncontrollably, but natural that sexual urges are without restraint and must have condoms? What about a diaper or shortage? I believe President Museveni of Uganda was quoted as saying, 'no foreign aid is needed for abstinence'.

I will admit that condoms are an escape. Condoms may be the only 'chance' for many women to escape from the predatory nature of men in a society that offers them little chance of protection by law, however the true cure will only come in a change of character. That change in character is found in Christ.

It is the slow acceptance of this fact that has allowed 'miracle cures' and the HIV/AIDS industry to develop in Kenya and other nations. Between the programs started for control of AIDS and the conferences dedicated to this illness, an industry has evolved from which government posts, and multiple NGO's (non governmental organizations).

Few are willing to admit that without food, water and minimal health care facilities, even free drugs for this illness will make a difference. The cure is in character, not condoms or curative drugs and therapy. However, Kenyan woman don't have the choices most would consider as basic human rights.

The rates of transmission of these diseases cause incredible consequences as husbands share their wives as in the Maasai tradition with any age mate who desires her. As easy as any given man or his friend can travel to the nearest town or village and sleep with a prostitute, they can travel just as easily home and sleep with their wife or their age mate's wife. She of course will bear children who will be at risk for carrying the same diseases she has gotten from her mate.

A study from 1987 by, the Centre for International Cooperation in Health and Development (CCISD) relates the high infectivity rate of this disease and the limited choices women have between choosing death and death. Death from the disease she derives from her husband, death from the disease she will transmit to her child and death for refusing her husband's advances as he can at anytime deny her the property rights of home, food, clothing and shelter.

Studies of the efficiency of peri-natal transmission have provided highly variable results. In Africa, the rate of vertical transmission from mother to child is of the order of 25 to 50 percent, with women who are more advanced clinically being more infectious for their offspring.

The incidence of AIDS is probably underestimated because of technical problems in the diagnosis of AIDS and HIV infection in infants. There is growing evidence that an as yet unknown proportion of peri-natally infected children do not become ill until the age of seven to ten years. This implies that it will take at least another decade before the full spectrum of morbidity and mortality of parentally acquired HIV infection is known.

The choices for a woman infected with HIV are terrible. In many cultures a woman's status, and often her material livelihood, depends on bearing children. In much of Africa, infant mortality rates are already so high that women expect up to half their infants to die before the age of five, the 50% risk of delivering an HIV-infected baby may not seem so bad.

This is the choice between death and death that many Kenyan woman face today. Tradition dictates many practices at the expense of common sense and death.

Ask people of the Maasai tribe of the decimation of their tribe by this same virus as they share wives and all of the venereal diseases that are passed around. Look around the Maasai compound of huts made of sticks and cow dung and see the hordes of flies alighting on the children and all of the foodstuffs which they put in their mouths.

As the government of Kenya and missionaries alike try to introduce these people to the 19th century, behold, they are content to return to the ante-deluvian, pre-wheel era of the cave man. Why? Because tradition dictates it.

It is important not to educate women in Kenya. Why? Because then they will become useful and productive. Tradition dictates that women are subservient in Kenya.

We know that they are the ones who spend more than 80% of the time with the children, yet no one understands how or why the children don't know how to read.

Tradition is important. As I stated before, in some tribes within Kenya, when you greet a married man you ask him; "How are the children?" This greeting includes the wife, so you don't have to ask "How is the wife?" Demeaning the woman is part of being Kenyan in many of the tribes. Tradition.

A 30-year-old unmarried man is referred to as a youth. The Swahili word is Kijana (pronounced kee-jah-nah). As long as he is unmarried, he is not considered whole. Demeaning the unmarried man is part of being Kenyan. Tradition. In Kenya, a woman is never a woman until she is married and has children. She is an Msichana (pronounced mm-see-cha-nah). Being childless is bad. This is tradition.

Now I know we have only recently begun to wrestle with some of these problems in America and even now wrestle with them in our many sub-cultures. But the impact this has on the intellectual and economic development of Kenya is much more devastating than we feel here in America. We can 'afford' to demean people, or so we think. Kenya does not have this luxury.

We throw away our soda bottles, or at best recycle them. They must collect the bottles and you must buy a soda. It's the way they've always done things. Our economy has the luxury of handing out food to women and children who cannot find food. This was not so of course until the mid 1940's when the great depression gave way to the great war. America was full of uneducated white and black women and children and poor folk until then. We have made some inroads, but I could see the issues clearly in Kenya as I still felt the pain in America.

In the mid 1960's when America declared its 'War on Poverty', there were millions of children going to bed and awakening without food. Even in the midst of an economic boom of the 1990's in the US, there are estimates of 600,000 Americans homeless every night according to the Washington Post (May 29, 1999) story on the crisis faced by HUD, with cities like Hartford Connecticut and Benton Harbor having poverty rates of 35-64%.

We are trying to eliminate these 'traditional values' of keeping people of color on the outer fringes of society. We have made some progress in America For instance you won't have this kind of thing happening in most parts of the US today We were visiting this family for the first time. He was a prominent local person in government service. She was an educated woman who ran the other family enterprises. They were well spoken and conversant on many topics other than those relevant to Kenya. They claimed to be Christians.

We were invited to church and then supper afterwards. It was a delightful Sunday. We spent the afternoon at their home which they were still in the midst of building. As we sat in the living room, we noticed an old man sitting on the porch outside. He was eating on the porch. He would stand every now and then, look at us through the window and smile and wave. This struck Kay and me as odd. What is this old man doing out there? "Who is that guy, I'm thinking? Don't you have a television or is this as good as it gets on Sunday afternoon?"

Our host and hostess note our glances and quizzical faces. "Oh! Say hello to my father" our host states proudly! Then he reverts to the tribal tongue and tells his father to stand and wave again and greet the guests. The father, gray haired and frail is smiling and not the least bit unnerved, stands like a 'jack in the box' toy and waves a cheery hello and says something in the local dialect and sits down again. Our host translates the greeting and sits down to finish eating. The old man disappears below the windowsill and we go on.

I look at Kay and she looks at me. This is not as good as television, but it is interesting. "What is that all about", I ask? "Why is your father sitting outside in the hot sun and we are inside under this cool roof?" I am thinking maybe he has bad table manners or hasn't bathed.

"Oh, that is just part of our custom," our host responds. "A father is never allowed in the son's home once the son has taken a wife."

"Oh." I said.

"My father's wife and my mother are both dead. He had two wives at one time, but they have both died and now he lives alone. I help him out and he lives nearby."

It was still customary in these parts of Kenya, as in most parts, for a husband to take multiple wives. This avoids the problems of adultery and divorce we have in the western nations. If a man needs sexual satisfaction from more than one woman, he simply marries her. The old tradition of having many wives to manage the farms is now replaced with the older tradition of....lust and many wives to meet the man's needs at mid-life crisis.

"Well, can't we invite him inside" I ask?

"No that is not possible, because it would violate the customs of our tribe and clan" my host responds.

I was deeply troubled by this. I could not understand how this man, my host, my friend could possibly relate the gospel of Christ to his father if he continued this practice? How can he tell his father that everyone is welcome into God's house, but not everyone is welcome into his house? How can he relate the love of Christ as being not respective of a person's socioeconomic, political, sexual, racial or educational background, when he himself is stuck acknowledging such practices by tradition?

How can we relate the importance of our children honoring their father and mother and continue to dishonor them this way? I believe this tradition has some relevance with regard to sexual morality and this must be acknowledged. However, whenever culture and tradition come in opposition to the Bible, they must give way. Anything which does not allow for unity of the body of Christ in truth serves no purpose in the kingdom.

Tradition does have its place. That place is always secondary to Biblical teaching. The man waving on the porch during dinner and the woman who must sleep and infect her brother in law with a killer disease are proof positive that tradition can kill the spirit and body.

LEARNING PATIENCE AND HUMILITY

I told you I already thought I was good enough for heaven. As I saw it, I was ready to go to heaven and lead things for the Lord. I just needed to pick out the kind of wings I needed and I would meet him on cloud number 9. Then I reminded him, 'don't be late! I have had enough of waiting down here.' That's when the Lord said, 'You need to learn patience and humility Michael. Go to Kenya!'

As many of the stories here relate, patience and humility are things I have yet to master. I think that is one reason I am still in Kenya. When I get it right, I will either return to the US or go on to glory.

One object lesson God gave me was shopping with my wife. Of course in 'up country' Kenya, that is anyplace other than an urban center, no real man would ever go shopping with his wife. Being from Putu land, I wouldn't be aware of such customs. I am just trying to impress my wife that I really am the sweet sensitive fellow I claim to be. So I follow behind her dutifully through the markets and shops. When she buys something in the crowded rows of vegetable vendors and artisans, I only offer my opinion if she asks for it.

"Oh yes I think those potatoes are a bit dirty too. No I wouldn't buy that fish, it has too many flies on it. I think you are

right, those are some nice bananas." Being a husband to a liber-
ated American woman is a challenge. "Oh nothing dear, I was
just thinking to myself about how liberating it is to be married
to you!"

The crowd of Kenyan men and women in the streets are staring at the two of us as we walk and talk. I am about four or five
paces behind Kay most of the time. I am struggling carrying
the bags of things she has foraged the market for. I think back,
"Aren't I supposed to be the hunter and gatherer in this setting?"

Some of the people snicker, but they all stare. This is strange
to them. They cannot figure out if I am Kay's houseboy or husband. I must be the houseboy because I keep running behind
her and she is doing all of the selection. What do I do now? Do
I dare succumb to the temptation to make Kay carry these bags
on her head and leave her here in the market place? Or should
I swallow my pride and keep on as a shining example of what a
real man in Christ is supposed to do to keep peace in my home (I
don't know about your home)?

If I don't swallow my pride, I might have to swallow my own
cooking which would be an even greater challenge.

One of my uncles says that one way to control my wife's
spending would be to let her shop in the tradition of Kenyan
women. If they buy it, they carry it. This would work well for us
as American men if we could do it and live to tell about it. Okay
fellas. The next time you are in K-Mart and your wife eyes a piece
of furniture, a nice cabinet or lawn chairs, just remind her you are
willing to pay for it if she will strap it on her head. Then duck.

I swallowed my pride and continued to pretend I was Kay's
houseboy. It was just one of many lessons in humility. Indeed,
we had a luscious meal from the items she had chosen.

Kenyans are a very patient people. They learn patience because
they have to persevere through so many circumstances which are
inhumane. I cared for a young boy who had learned patience.

He first presented to our hospital with a tumor on the side of his thigh the size of a small lemon. We biopsied it and found it to be a cancer. He was about 12 years old at the time. We advised its removal and possible radiation therapy in Nairobi. The family decided they would seek a second opinion from the medicine man. They returned to see us one year later. The medicine man had failed.

Upon their return, the tumor was the size of a large watermelon. It was bleeding and foul smelling. It was so large the boy could not walk. It was so massive with swelling and infection that the pain would not allow him to sleep. It was so rank in odor that he could not eat. It bled so much that he was even too weak to sit up for long periods of time. This boy had learned patience through perseverance.

I did a disarticulation of this boy's hip, removing the entire hip and leg from the socket. I had to advise the family that this was only palliative because the tumor had no doubt spread from the time of his initial diagnosis. God was teaching me that if this boy, who, despite the pain evident on his face and in his voice never shed a tear. As I cared for him over these several weeks, I saw him accept and praise Christ as Lord and Savior. It is obvious, I had yet a lot to learn about perseverance and patience.

I am still learning. I keep comparing my humility with others. It is obvious in doing so, I have not arrived.

MAASAI LAND MINES

I had a friend tell me he didn't like being around dogs or birds. He didn't know whether to look up or look down. I have often thought about this as I traverse the compounds and roadways we travel in Kenya. The dogs aren't so bad and the birds seem to leave you alone. But those cows!

I know that the cow is an important entity to people in rural communities in America and around the world. I just don't understand why God made them to be so messy.

I listen to the reports on the radio of the dog patrols in New York's Central Park. Imagine that. Fining people for what their dogs do naturally. What would these police do if they came to Bomet. They would have to use the paper for citations for other practical things.

We had the opportunity to see first hand the effect of uncontrolled cattle. We visited a Maasai manyatta. This is the homestead of these nomadic people. It basically is an encampment surrounded by sticks and thorn bushes with numerous dwellings inside. This one was the size of a baseball diamond. The sticks and thorn bushes are piled high and thick to keep the predators out. I am talking about the four footed predators which growl and walk off with one of your goats or small calves in their mouth. This is not the kind of encampment where you hook your car and trailer up to the water and power.

The homes are numerous, about 12 in all. There is one man for this manyatta. He has one wife in each of these homes. He can go into any of these homes at any time and have his needs met. That is unless he sees a spear outside of the house. That indicates that one of his age mates is inside having his needs met. He in turn must find another place to hang his hat or plant his spear as it were.

As we approach the entrance to the compound I notice a small cow pie. I think "I should've been more careful parking. I certainly don't want to step in that and have that stuff in the car when we get ready to leave." I alert Keturah about it because she is only wearing sandals. "Be careful sweetheart, there is some cow doo-doo here!" This stuff is everywhere like land mines!

We walk into the compound. Kay is close behind me, careful not to step on one of these Maasai land mines herself. We are through the gates and we notice the homes. They are about five feet tall and appear to be made of the same sticks that the fence is made of. There appears to be some strange mortar holding these together. Even the roof appears to have some kind of brown spackle. Spackle?!? That's not spackle. That's.....!

I turn to explain to Kay who is still in the gateway with a look of disbelief and grief on her face. "Oh no," I think "she's been hit!"

I move towards her in an effort to extract her foot from the camouflaged booby trap and she shouts at me. "Michael, do you know what we are walking in"

I look down. To my dismay the whole compound is made up of nothing but land mines. These land mines are in various states of disintegration but many of them are still active as evidenced by the flies circling and landing on them. Keturah is clinging to Kay for dear life. Sandals are no match for this kind of army maneuver, she needs boots.

I turn to our Maasai guide and he smiles at me. I don't want to be offensive so I just walk on behind him quietly, expecting Kay and the others to follow. As we approach the houses I notice that the stuff I mistook for spackle is the same substance we are standing in. That's interesting I muse. I wonder how they put it up there There are flies everywhere. Every one of the kids must have at least one dozen flies on their faces. There are at least twice that many hanging on their bodies and limbs.

It starts to rain and so we hurry into the house, lest we get something clean and refreshing on our bodies. The house is dark and smoky. It also smells like...., spackle. As we enter the vestibule we notice a small cubicle. Well for real, the whole house is nothing more than a small cubicle, smaller than the average American kitchen. So this would be a small cubicle within a cubicle. I ask our guide, what is that for.

He then goes on to explain to me the entire phenomenon of why there is so much to avoid on the grounds of the compound. "You see when the cattle are out during the day, we can watch for the lions that want to kill them. But during the night, we must bring the cattle into the compound to protect them. This small area of the house is where we keep the young animals, sometimes calves, sometimes and goats. They stay with us in the house at night to keep warm. By the way, can I get you something to drink"

The rain stops and we are allowed to exit the abode. Our eyes readjust to the sun and of course, the flies have been congregating in greater numbers outside. We notice that we are the only ones shooing them away.

I see the open sores on bodies of the children on which flies are landing. I see the pus running from one child's eyes as the flies land on it and then alight on the baby she is carrying on her back. This is indeed a challenge.

As we leave the compound we notice several women are down on their hands and knees working with something that looks oddly familiar. I ask our guide "What is going on"

"Since the rain has come, it has made the cow dung moist. The women are now mixing it with their hands so they can smear it on the houses to keep the walls from cracking and falling apart. Would you like to meet one of these women"

We are now a learned group. We recognize this minefield has no map. We just have to make a straight line to the car and a hasty exit.

THERE ARE NO CRAZY PEOPLE IN AFRICA.

He stood before me covered with dirt and grit. He was about 30 years old. His clothes were torn and dirty and there was blood on one sleeve. He didn't seem to be in pain as he spoke calmly holding one arm in the other. Then as I looked more closely I saw, he was literally holding one arm in the other. His right arm had been nearly amputated just above the elbow and was held in place by a small island of skin. I looked at his face again and saw no obvious sign of physical pain, but I did see anguish.

I had gone to work that morning after having a good night's sleep in a comfortable bed. I had awakened and kissed my wife, shaved and had a nice hot shower. I went to work with both of my hands and feet and had put in a reasonable amount of time with my patients. Now I am confronted with this man.

This man had no doubt gone to sleep on wooden cot in a small shack near the hospital. He most likely had only a handful of corn to eat. His wife was probably back on the farm with their four or five hungry half naked children.

The only water he had seen today was that running on the side of the road, some of it being lapped up by the cows and contaminated with the garbage of the road.

This man had gone to work that morning with two arms and by mid afternoon at work in the rock quarry an accident had happened. The rocks above him started to slide and without warning, his right arm was pinned beneath a heavy boulder, crushed just above the elbow and nearly amputated. There in the quarry he called for the help of his coworkers and they freed him and brought him to the hospital. There was no way to salvage the arm. By mid-afternoon he was asleep and I completed the amputation. By mid-week, he was released.

The hospital bill however was still pending. There was no workmen's compensation for this man. There is no Kenyan equivalent of handicap rights we have in America. This man would have to pay for the surgery out of his meager earnings of 50 shilling per day, or about $1 per day. The entire cost was probably $100. How did he stop from going crazy?

I was sure there were no crazy people in Africa. I thought that with all of the stresses here, no one can afford a neurosis. If you are neurotic or psychotic, there is no way to treat you for long. Even those with seizure disorders and other severe neurological disorders go without medicines for most of their lives. Why pay to treat a disorder which is not going to kill you? Food is more essential than medicine. Ignore the crazies. They are not there.

My biases not withstanding, there are crazy people in Africa. In Psychiatric News (reported in Psychiatric News Main Frame 7/99) Harold Eist, M.D., past president of the American Psychiatric Association states that "...psychiatric illnesses will become an increasing global burden, with major depression ranked second only to heart disease by the year 2000. Schizophrenia will affect 25 million people in the poorer nations by the year 2000, a 45 percent increase since 1985." He attributes much of this to the explosive urbanization and inadequate services for the mentally ill. I am not sure how Dr. Eist came to his conclusions as there are no psychiatrists practicing in rural Kenya and in the cities, the poor can't afford to seek psychiatric consultation. I have come to recognize there is real mental illness.

There still is a noted racial bias in diagnoses and treatment of all sorts of illnesses in America. The American College of Cardiology at its 48th annual meeting in Detroit noted a racial bias against black patients, resulting in death rates twice that for whites. Similar studies were reported by the American Medical Association which noted a bias not accounted for by income, or insurance.

I remember growing up if a black person was crazy there were just that 'crazy'. None of us could afford a psychiatrist who could give us diagnoses such as manic-depression or agorophobia, or aerophobia. We didn't have to worry about fear of flying in an airplane when I was growing up because black folk were too poor to fly. This may seem a bit contrived, but we were actually made

to believe for the longest time that we were too stupid or uncivilized to be crazy. Many 'scientific' studies attested to the fact
that the African slave in America was not capable of having real
mental illness.

In "Racism and Mental Health" by Willie and Kramer,
American psychiatrist Dr. Isaac Ray lamented that "When it
appeared that the Black had less mental illness throughout the
United States, this fact was explained as the natural result of his
uncivilized nature." Dr. Jarvis in the same book notes "slavery,
although 'refusing many of the hopes and responsibilities which
the free, self thinking and self acting enjoy and sustain, had the
advantage to the slave of saving him from some of the liabilities
and dangers of self destruction.

The false position of the Northern freedman had a bad effect
on his own character."   Dr. A.. Witmer is quoted as acknowledging the golden age of slavery which when it ended cause a
dramatic rise in insanity amongst the African;"previous to their
emancipation, the health and morals of the slaves were carefully
preserved and inebriety, excessive venrery and venereal diseases
were closely guarded against; since their liberation...., untutored
in a knowledge of the world, and without a sound philosophy or
religion deeper seated than the emotions to sustain them in ad-
versity, many minds have failed under the constant strain of their
advancing civilization."

These racist ideas about mental illness were prevalent even
when I was growing up. We were considered too poor or too
stupid to be crazy. It was only when we moved up north and
started associating with intelligent and cultured white people that
the blinders fell off of our eyes and we were blessed with insanity
as they were.

Hence, I had laid my same biases on Africans. I was sure they
were too poor or too unlearned to be crazy because they like me
were black. Until I started seeing the number of young people

coming in dying from suicides and attempted suicides. This was occurring at a rate of at least two to three per month. Children, young adults, teens, all taking lethal doses of insecticides or anti-malaria medicines. Many of them died enroute to the hospital or shortly thereafter. We did manage to save some. Then I knew that Africans could be crazy, but just too poor to afford treatment.

We have had a hard time distinguishing demonic possession from schizophrenia. Our hospital chaplains always defer to our western models of schizophrenia because it sounds newer and better and you can give someone injections for it. But I often wonder, what do they do when they go home and see crazy people? Do they pray for them and chant and send for the medicine man or witch doctor?

Dr. Frank Njenga came to Tenwek one day to lecture on Psychiatric illnesses in rural Kenya. Dr. Njenga is a Kenyan Psychiatrist, well renown in Kenya and around the world. He has spoken on a variety of radio shows including the BBC and is often quoted in the Kenya press and medical journals.

Dr. Njenga went on to explain to us that of course poor people in Kenya can go crazy. How else could we explain the amount of alcohol abuse in our area? How else, he further elucidated, could we account for the spousal abuse and child sexual abuse which occurred? There was a tremendous amount of perversion, as much as in any western culture, right there in our midst. Kenyans faced the stresses of life and managed them the same way we do in America.

Dr. Njenga's explanation for the resurgence of polygamy in Kenya was it was often the men's way of managing their mid-life crisis. It allowed them to meet their needs and be within culturally acceptable bounds. This is not adultery, but polygamy. This makes the divorce statistics look good.

I began to recognize the patients who were 'crazy' then. I took notice that the man who hung himself in the hospital ward because he was diagnosed with AIDS was more than just transiently depressed. The other man who hung himself at home after being caught in sexual relations with a cow was just as 'crazy'. And of course the man who jumped from the third story of the hospital building because he saw something in a dream one night was more than just off center as he saw people chasing him trying to set him on fire in his nightmare. These guys were just the tip of the insane iceberg of people on the ward who would lay awake at night screaming and on occasion bite the nurses and other caregivers.

No reasonable person could imagine there are no 'crazy' people in Africa if we consider the mass slaughter of over one half million people in Rwanda in 1995. I saw similarities to this as I took care of the remaining female family member who survived a homemade massacre. A young man, her brother took a machete to his mother, father, several brothers and sisters, slaughtering them all on the family compound before being captured, brutalized and killed by the police.

No one can reason that insanity is not part of the Kenyan landscape as one witnesses a crowd of everyday working people in the major cities and towns of Kenya, suddenly descend on a young boy or girl who has snatched a purse or stolen a piece of fruit. This crowd of everyday 'good and sane' people will stop on their way to work, or lunch or mid-day stroll and mete out vengeance on one of the over 45,000 the street children in Nairobi. The child is stomped, beaten and sometimes burned to death. This is not sanity.

Crazy' people wander the hills of the highlands and the streets of the cities, talking to themselves, naked or half naked, hallucinating and experiencing another dimension of reality. We call it schizophrenia. I am not sure what the common Kenyan thinks of it. Many think it is just demon possession. As for the difference between demonic possession and schizophrenia, which was a question raised by one of our chaplains, Dr. Njenga responded; "render unto Caesar what is Caesar's , I am not here to define, or confine your faith."

You can be crazy in Africa, it just costs more.

BOOK FOUR/MORE PERSONAL FAILINGS/ CHALLENGES WHO SPAT ON ME?/BEING A NIGGER IN AFRICA

Being a nigger is something you get used to. I had grown up accustomed to walking down the streets of Chicago and being yelled at by angry white people. I didn't think twice about it when my family was chased off the beach by an angry white mob as the police told my mother there was nothing they could do.

One beautiful day in Chicago I walked along the street on my way home and felt a warm moist feeling on my face. It was slimy. I looked up and saw some white boys on the city bus laughing as the spittle they had launched at me dripped down my face and onto my neck. I thought this was the last time I could be made to feel like a nigger.

But then I went to Africa. Africa, the land of my forefathers. Africa the land of wonderful heritage and promise. It was upon our first arrival to Tenwek in 1990. We had only been in Kenya for a few weeks and the riots were already starting.

The hospital staff usually met in the meeting room to praise God and pray. This room also served as a place for teaching classes for the nurses and physician sign in for morning report. Now it was being used for more practical things in the sight of the conveners. It was used to call for the immediate death of the matron, the head nurse and her children.

Many of these same people who praised the Lord on Sunday and prayed to Him on Wednesday prayer service, were using the same room to call for the murder and mutilation of a woman solely because she dare discipline someone who was of their tribe and she was a foreigner, a Ugandan.

They furthermore called for the death of or eviction of any missionary who dare stand in their way. The staff was told to support them by going on strike. It didn't matter that the only people who would suffer from the lack of care were their own countrymen, neighbors and clans men. For several hours that night, the patients went unattended as the staff called for the head of the matron.

Someone must be made to pay for this insult. And the hospital meeting room and prayer room was as good a place as any to advocate death and abolishment of the accused.

This incident was resolved when Dr. David Stevens went into the meeting room and announced that anyone who was not at work at the assigned time performing their assigned duties would be without assignment, i.e. would be fired or sacked as the local vernacular has it. With that said, tensions eased a bit, however, the strain was felt around the mission compound the entire evening and the next day.

Now the matron had been hidden in one of the missionary homes. Her children, however, were being cared for by one of the local folk. The problem was, how to get her children out of the local people's hands without getting them hurt. The solution; 'use Kay and Michael Johnson, the new missionaries who blend in so well. No one will know them!' So that was the plan. Kay and I were summoned to make a preemptive strike under cover of dark. This is one reason it is sometimes good to be dark in Africa.

We went to the home, avoiding eye contact with any of the local people, lest they recognize us as the black white people. We informed the baby sitter that someone had sent us to pick up the kids. She didn't ask who, or why. She handed the kids over to us without hesitation. I am sure she did not expect a tip from the matron for her special care. We then took the children to their mother who was hiding in the missionary home. Several days later, she was taken to Uganda by missionaries.

This was our introduction to the work of full time missions in Kenya, East Africa in 1990. It only served as an appetizer for some of the surprises to come later.

For the next three days, matron hid out in one of the missionary's home. The local people posted signs all around the compound threatening missionary sympathizers and any out of tribes people with harm and death. I felt just like I felt when I was spat upon and called a nigger back home in America. I felt unable to protect my wife as she told me of the man who met her on the road with a machete that night as she was returning home during this ongoing unrest. As I said, someone had posted signs around the mission compound that no out of tribes people were to be allowed as they were intent on killing them all. Kay was definitely out of tribes.

I sat in a meeting one day in the hospital board room couple of years later. It was 1992 after the introduction of multi-party politics to Kenya. We were meeting with the chief of Bomet and the soldiers which had been placed there for our protection from the rioting community around us. We were in danger and so were our 'out of tribes' nurses. They had been threatened with bodily harm and were afraid to leave their homes to even report to work at the hospital.

Kay and I were warned that we should not leave the compound unless we were accompanied by white missionaries. Our lives would be in danger on these country roads. No one would ever take us for Americans. Rather they would suspect we were the evil other tribe. The bad people. The niggers, in their eyes.

Soldiers were called in to protect us and the nurses. I was called into the boardroom to give a pep talk to the nurses. The nurses were all talking about leaving. They were afraid for their lives. They were ready to leave and at this point they were the mainstay of our patient care. I had to give them an 'I have a dream' like speech. The missionaries asked me to step in to offer this assistance. We sat around the big table and looked at each other.

The chief, the soldiers, the District Commissioner and his Administrative Police, the missionaries, the out of tribe nurses and waited for someone to say something. The District Commissioner started. He wanted to know what all of the hub-bub was about. Why did we need this meeting?

When we told him our nurses feared for their lives, he was amazed, or at least he pretended to be. I remember this 'amazement' when we would see George Wallace and Bull Connor say they could not understand that the 'nigras' was unhappy.

We talked with the nurses and then I had to tell them, they could not go. I told them that if they left Tenwek they would set "integration" behind for many years. I told them that I had felt the fear they felt and the rejection they knew from being different and being niggers. I knew what it was like to be spat upon because I was spat upon in the past.

I was later to meet every one of those nurses one by one and convince all but one of eight to stay on at Tenwek. She later returned after a few years of being away. I know now, who spat on me and I know why they did. The enemy did and God allowed it so that I could use that experience for a time like this.

I liked being a secret agent and also I found out that being spat upon can come in handy sometimes. In addition I found that being a nigger in Africa was the same as in America. We were hated by people and suspected of evil just because we did not look exactly like them or talk like them.

We were considered niggers here because we dared to question the wisdom and goodness of the dominant culture. We were dangerous outsiders just like Martin Luther King was, whenever he would visit a community and advocate justice and equality.

We had to justify our existence in this land of our heritage just as we had to justify our existence in the land of our birth.

BLACK MAN, BLACK HAT, BLACK COAT AND BLACK CAR

Talk about stereotypes, this really happened! I had come home from Kenya after 7 weeks of serving in Jesus name in 1987. It was our second short-term mission trip. I was proud. I was humble. I was proud to have been so humble. While I was away, someone had stolen the license plates from my brand new black Bonneville. They like to do things like that in Philadelphia communities, even in the suburbs!

Since Kay had returned three weeks earlier than I, she had inquired of the police in Upper Darby where we were living at that time. We were still the only black folk on the block. The police told Kay to make a cardboard mockup of the plates and place it in the back window. She did so and used my car for the three weeks I was away.

When we had first moved to this community, our black friends were afraid to visit us because it was apparent we didn't know, we weren't supposed to move there. 'Black people don't live in Upper Darby' they would explain to us! We were a tourist phenomenon for some time as black people from Philadelphia would ride past our home just to see if it was true that some of them had made the move across the tracks.

Well, I returned home to this community after spending those few weeks in Kenya, proud of what God had done through me. I had carried out the great commission, without receiving a monetary compensation in return. Now I was back at home, where I belonged.

I attended church where I was chairman of deacons that Sunday. Then on Monday morning, started up the car, drove the kids to their private school in Philadelphia, made rounds at the hospitals and was headed home, when I decided I should stop and get an application for new plates. I had neglected to take my wallet that morning. However, since the place for renewing plates was just down the street from my home, and since all of the police knew me as the only black guy in the neighborhood, I was surely safe to park my car, go across the street and pick up this application. I did so.

I came back to my car and got ready to get in it. As I pulled out my key to open the door, I was approached by a police car from the neighboring suburb of Melbourne. Now Melbourne and Upper Darby are millimeters apart on my side of town. Literally, across the street from each other. These municipalities recently settled a civil rights suit against them most of the traffic citations written in this 99.999% white community were written against non-white motorists.

I think the officer saw an opportunity. He got out of his squad car. He asked me for my ID. I had none, but my house was just a block and one half away and after all, "What is the problem officer, I asked?"

"This vehicle has been reported stolen." was his reply.

"Well, that's impossible sir, because it is my car and I know the plates are missing, but I have here in my hand an application for new plates!"

To make a long story short, he cuffed me, and put me in the back of his car. I was scared. It was about 10:00 on a Monday morning on the middle of a busy thoroughfare in suburban Philadelphia. As he was pushing my head into the car, I yelled out to a young black man on the street to call my wife and gave him the number. I wasn't sure what would happen to me, but I was scared.

The Holy Spirit bade me not resist this man. He kept bringing to remembrance the words of Christ on the cross; (Luke 23:34) "Father forgive them, for they know not what they do." I did not want to be another statistic of another black man who spoke too loudly or moved to fast and they had to 'put him down.'

I know driving that beautiful black Bonneville and wearing that black leather coat and black hat was a bit much for this white officer. He had to do something to spoil this proud nigger's day. Well, he tried his best. If it were not for Jesus, this man could have done a lot more.

The secretary at the police station was a neighbor of ours. As I was led into the station, which was just two blocks from my house, she looked at me. She never said a mumbling word.   I guess she was trying to be like Jesus, you know,' mute before my accusers.' Well, it might be kind of hard for a white woman to defend a black man in a black coat and a black hat driving a black car which he had parked on her block and the place where he lived with his family for five and one half years.

Kay came and got me. She had all the necessary documents. She greeted our neighbor who sat behind the desk. She remained mute to Kay and pretended not to know either of us.

A few weeks later, I wrote the arresting officer a letter. I told him that I recognized what moved him to do such a thing. I told him that Jesus could fix it for him if He would allow it. I don't know what came of that letter, but I do know I grew from the experience.

I grew enough to try it again. This time I carried my wallet. I was traveling even further back in time. I was headed to what I had heard was KKK country. I carried my wallet and made sure I stayed within the law while driving. This time in Marion Indiana, the site of the last officially openly sanctioned KKK lynching of two black men in the US in 1930.

I drove to World Gospel Mission Headquarters in beautiful Marion Indiana. I just recently saw a picture in a political science book of a black man being lynched in Marion Indiana in 1930. I had just been accepted as a full time missionary. I had never been to the headquarters and I thought it might be interesting to see how they would respond to the black man in the black coat and black hat driving the black car.

I know this first hand. The person who relates this to me is a dear friend and brother of mine. He tells me that when I pulled into the parking lot of the mission headquarters I scared him. He went on to tell me he inquired "Who is that black man?' as I walked up the driveway. He was informed "that is Dr. Johnson, our new missionary!" What a surprise.

I reportedly started making waves immediately. I wanted to know why there were no black people on staff at this place. "How can you minister to people of color when you have none working in your midst?" I learned to be direct from my mom and my aunt who believe in taking no prisoners.

As I said before, there are reasons in history why black people don't want to travel with white agencies over large bodies of water. There are many other reasons why there are not many black men in black hats and coats driving black cars working in all white mission agencies. They are afraid of us.

Somehow many white mission agencies have located their offices outside of the sphere of most black Americans. They are afraid of going into black churches because they fear the racial divide as well. The discomfort of worshipping in a different way with different people is real. The fear of some physical harm is real.   Racial profiling is not limited to police forces. We must work together to overcome the fears which paralyze our working together.

I STILL SING THE BLUES

The little black girl and little black boy are walking along in the park together. They are about 8 years old and their understanding of the American culture is just beginning to show. It is the mid 1950's. A note here for those of you who don't know who Joe Louis was. Joe Louis was the black American of boxing fame who held the world heavyweight championship longer than any man in history, from 1937 onward, defending the title successfully 25 times, 20 times by knockout. He was known as the Brown Bomber

Back to the little boy and girl, and the conversation ensues with the black boy proudly stating; "I ain't never been in any white person's house before!" His companion the little girl replies;" Well it is just like being in a black person's home, except for one thing." The boy takes notice and asks; "What's that?"

She replies "In a white person's home they have a picture of the Pope and in the black person's home they have a picture of Joe Louis!" The boy unabashed shoots back; "Well, I bet Joe Louis could whip the Pope!" This is a scene from the movie Polly a story about settling community differences. The differences in this community are between black and white people. Suffice it to say, we still have those differences in American mission work.

I was glad to have brought out my B.B. King and Albert King music collection to Kenya. I just happen to like the blues. I grew up in Chicago and went to the blues concerts as a kid.

Here I am in the deep hinterlands of Kenya, listening to that sorrowful guitar and the wailing voice and feeling pretty good about it. I decide to sing along and that helps. I like the music and the memories of the Kings. You know, B.B. King and Albert King. I even like some of the political and business savvy of Don King, though I can't do my hair like he does his. B. B. and Albert sing songs reflecting the memories and miseries spoken of, and lived by Martin Luther King and of course Rodney King. These are the Kings we think of in black America. We don't include Elvis as worthy of being included in this list of Kings even if he is still alive.

Now of course in black American Christian circles we know Jesus is the King of kings. As black Americans we identify Jesus the human in a different light than white Americans. This is of course a generalization, but there are certain things which appeal to us. In Isaiah 53, He is described as a man of sorrows. He is despised and rejected. He is so unsightly that we don't even want to gaze upon Him. It pleased God that He should suffer. God laid upon Him the iniquity of us all. He was wounded for our transgressions. His Father forsook Him in His hour of agony. This is really the kind of lyrics that make up the blues.

To understand the blues is to watch Jesus cry out to his tormentors; "Please why don't you leave me alone!" Then He cries out to His Father; "Please don't leave me alone!"

We were a people of sorrows, having been stolen and sold as property and when too old to work, discarded as garbage. We were despised and rejected even though we built the infrastructure of the nation. We fought and died in every one of this nation's wars as segregated units until the Korean War in 1950. We were considered unsightly as our images didn't begin to grace billboards, television or magazines until a lot of people had boycotted, rioted and died.

I really believe Jesus would most likely have enjoyed the blues. He could certainly appreciate these lyrics from B.B. and his guitar, Lucille; "I laid in the ghetto flats, cold and numb, I heard the rats tell the bed bugs, to give the roaches some and everybody wants to know, why I sing the blues, I said I've been around a long time, you know I've paid my dues" I don't believe there were no bed bugs and roaches in the manger where Christ was born. I would tend to think it was a bit cold and numb. James Brown (godfather of soul) says when he was growing up, they were so poor the roaches would go next door to eat. I believe Jesus the Christ knew this kind of poverty.

Somehow we have forgotten that Jesus was both human and divine. We forget that this King of kings was born in a barn and laid in an animal trough. Oh yes the Christ in Him recognized the noble birth, but the Jesus part of him was bitten by the fleas in the barn as his mother and father chased the rats away from the feeding trough. Jesus knew what it was like to be poor and outcast. I think Jesus would've enjoy the blues if they had been invented then.

Jesus went to places where people were more likely to sing the blues. He spent time with poor people in the slums of the cities and in the outskirts of the town where water was sparse and diseases were rampant. He saw hunger and pain. He saw women rejected and spat upon for being caught in adultery, while powerful men used them to make political gain. Jesus saw the incurable maniacs and the religious outcasts crying to be made whole. Our Savior touched untouchable people and allowed them to touch him. Jesus understood just how blue people can feel because He was born in such circumstances.

In our desire to purify the gospel from the dirges of the common man, we have somehow made it not palatable for the common man. We fail to recognize that the early church restricted the Bible from the common man and we have now made the Bible to be interpreted only by those whose hands are holy enough, not filled with the common dirges of the day.

We black people in America sang the blues more than we read the newspaper. There was a reason for this. Singing the blues was never illegal. Singing the blues could never get you burned at the stake or hung from a tree. Singing the blues was safe.

Singing the blues didn't cost nothing, when you had nothing. You could sing the blues without putting out any money. Singing the blues was cheap. You could sing the blues when you had no light. You can't read the paper when you don't have light, but the blues can be sung in a dirt floor cabin in Mississippi even if there is no oil for the lantern.

Singing the blues could never get you deported or cause you to live in exile, like W.E.B. Dubois and Richard Baldwin and Paul Robeson who felt living in exile the only alternative to being rejected in America because their thoughts were considered too radical.

We black people in America liked to sing the blues because it was one of the few things we could afford to do which did not endanger our lives or our families. When black Americans sang the blues it was not about singing a song. It was about life.

When black slaves were singing they were supposed to be happy. This was what the slave masters generally thought. A happy slave is a safe slave, one you can trust not to be involved in rebellion or mayhem. Singing a song in church meant you were trying to please God and seek peace. Singing a song in a brothel meant you were drunk and too content to upset the system. Singing was safer than reading.

That in itself accounts for the relative lack of black intellectual writers and the relative excess of black inspirational songwriters. It is always safer to sing than it is to think if you are black. One led to success, the other often led to death. In the 'good old days' many white people in the old south were killed because they dared teach a 'nigra' to read. No one dare teach him how to write. This speaks for much of black American intellectual impotence today. Please don't get me wrong. Black Americans have and continue to have a tremendous pool of intellectual talent. However, the emphasis on entertainment and sports is evident in our sub-culture in America and there is no denying this.

People are still amazed when a black man can express himself intellectually. They are rarely amazed that he can sing, dance, act or play basketball or other sports. It is what we have been allowed to do and hence we do it well. On the mission field, my fellow missionaries are amazed frequently when I don't play basketball with them. I tell them "I don't know how!"

My wife even laughs at me when we do those aerobic exercises with the videotapes because I can't keep time or rhythm with the group leader on the screen. She shouts; "Don't step on my toes! Move to the left! Go in the next room!" I have taken to being a closet aerobic dancer these days, because she describes me as 'rhythmically challenged.'

My brother has just completed his second book and is working on his third. He is now a tenured professor at Central Michigan University. He has overcome the tendency to be non-intellectual against the advice of his high school advisors who told him he was not college material. Anyway, he can't play basketball either. I don't know about his dancing.

I still like the blues. I recognize the blues in Russian folklore as written by Tolstoy, who tells of the suffering of his people under the czars and dictators of his day. I hear the blues in composers such as Rimsky Korsakov's composition of Scheherazade, where the violin soloist renders a melody that breaks your heart. Anton Dvorzak the Czechoslovakian studied black American spiritual music on his visit to the US in the 19th century. He then wrote the Symphony for the New World and attributed the success of this work to the rhythms and sounds he found in this and native American music. Anton dug the blues!

I hear the blues in the guitar work of Carlos Santana on his album Caravanserai as it sweeps the room with the weeping of his people of descent. When Willie Nelson sang with Ray Charles, I recognized that Country Western music is nothing more than the blues with a cowboy hat. The blues is not a single type of music, it is a common experience to mankind. I believe Jesus knew the blues because 'He heard the rats tell the bed bugs to give the roaches some.'

I asked a physician friend of mine how many of the families in Kenya can afford to feed, clothe, educate, house and immunize their children. He responded, maybe 20 percent. In his estimation 80% of the people of Kenya have to decide on which basics of life they could do without, because there is not much you can do on the equivalent of 80 American cents per day. That ain't nothing but the blues.

In one song, B.B. King goes on to say; 'I brought you a brand new Ford and you said, "I want a Cadillac"; I bought you a ten dollar dinner and you said "Thanks for the snack"; I let you live in my penthouse and you said; "It was just a shack"; I gave you seven children and now you want to give them back" That is rejection. The blues is about rejection and how to laugh at the rejection you feel as a person and a people.

Kenyan's know rejection. They have been rejected by their conquerors, the British and now their entire culture has been rejected as a worthless thing as the west continues to invade them with technology and new ideas. Jesus knew rejection as He hung on the cross and His disciples abandoned Him to the whims of His accusers and then the ultimate blues, abandoned by His own Father (Mark 15:34) If that ain't the blues, I don't know what is.

It is no doubt that I have had the same attitude towards Kenyans that I perceive white Americans to have towards me. Can they think? Are they capable?

Can they lead and plan? Do they only have the ability to mimic and follow? Can they create? Do they only have the ability to farm and do heavy labor? Are they innately rhythmic?

The challenge for white mission agencies is how do they incorporate people of other cultures into their programs. How can they possibly minister to other cultures in a more effective way than they are doing. My answer is to start understanding and accepting the other cultures right in your own back yard, or next door (that is if you haven't moved from the 'changing' neighborhood). Black Americans can sense the blues in people who are singing not out of joy but out of misery. We can sense the private pain a whole lot more, because we still face it and are sensitive to it. We can be an effective part of a team that means to take Christ to the nations.

If we want to bring other people into missions, we must recognize their gifts of serving come from their experiences. We can no more ask them for their gifts and leave out their experiences than God could ask Christ to be only flesh and blood. Jesus was able to speak of heaven because He knew it as home. He spoke not of someplace He was heading, but also as a place He had been.

We can no more judge the genuineness of someone's testimony than we can the genuineness of their experience. Since the one blind man who was healed with the spit of Jesus (Mark 8:32) did not know that the other was healed by just the master's touch (Matthew 9:28) , it does not invalidate either experience.

God has promised He would give us 'treasures of darkness and hidden riches of secret places.'(Isaiah 45:3). The blues are such a secret place wherein we can find such treasures of darkness. God got glory in the cross, another treasure in darkness in a secret place. Who else would look for treasure in such a place? He was further glorified as Jesus was in the dark grave. The ultimate glory of course came out of this dark place at resurrection morning.

We must be careful to not put so many astringents on the gospel. We make it so heavenly good that it is of no earthly use. Keep on singing the blues.

MISSIONARY PRAISE POLICE

I recognize the importance of rules and doctrines. Just referring to our mission's history of its work in Kenya, it becomes obvious that there were some very strange activities going on when they arrived. Many of the religious rites, marriage, funerals and even births were celebrated with more than just a touch of animism and ancestral worship. Witch doctors were prominent and feared. Blood sacrifice to the gods was not uncommon.

The missionaries in my opinion, correctly recognized the impediment some of these practices posed to establishing Christianity. Polygamy, female circumcision and other rituals, such as burying the dead facing a certain way to avoid the spirits coming into the home, were common and some posed certain health risks to the population. To allow these to continue unabated would make evangelization difficult. Leveritic wife inheritance is still practiced in many communities and this alone has been not only an impediment to the gospel but a challenge in the era of AIDS and other sexually transmitted diseases.

The missionary zeal to make conformity as they saw it accounts for the loss of many indigenous forms of worship in many of the churches in Kenya today. On a given Sunday morning service, if you closed your eyes, you might think you were in the hills of Methodist Kentucky instead of the hills of Kenya. The Kenyans in our churches were told not to use drums or other traditional instruments. Hence, the guitar and the piano and other instruments of reed and brass are considered holy unto the Lord, but tambourines and other percussion instruments are to this day considered ungodly by many of those with whom we worship.

I remain particularly sensitive to the idea of someone monitoring my worship of the Almighty. We as black Americans were subject to this kind of thing in history. In many states we were not allowed to gather without a white man present until the mid

20th century. This included our worship services also. Praise police scare me.

I was approached by one of the Kenyan church leaders after having brought some of my Philadelphia friends to Kenya. It appears these black Americans had upset some of our Kenyan pastors and some of the missionaries as well. It had something to do with their style of worship. All of that hand clapping and shouting and crying and hand waving and jumping up and down and saying hallelujah, was having a distinct effect. It was directly opposite of what these folks had been taught was the right way to worship.

My Kenyan pastor friend was coming to me in sincerity and truth to tell me that I must not invite these people again, or if I did, I must tell them how to conduct themselves. Of course I had the exact opposite comments from the Kenyan staff and community who attended these services. "Please send us more people like this" was the response I got from them. "We had no idea that Americans could worship like this. We had no idea your people were so much like us."

The Praise Police had struck again. It was well known that on the Tenwek compound, certain meetings were considered fringes of Christianity because the people decided to use drums and tambourines, shout and jump. It was felt this represented a possible return to the practices of old where chicken blood was an element of praise and a certain white goat was given to the medicine man or a spotted cow to the witch doctor.

Though the intent may be good, the method strangulates any chance of self-determination or pride. God saves Kenyans from their sins just like He saves us from our sins. However, God would never have us totally imitate another culture in order to find our freedom in Christ. If our freedom in Christ must be monitored and kept in check, it is not freedom. As the proverb goes; 'If a man gives you freedom, it is not yours.'

I do believe that often times we as black Americans are a bit too emotional in our praise. We often equate our emotion with faith. Dr. Martin Luther King stated in his famous oratory entitled 'A knock at Midnight'; "our churches often have more religion in their hands and feet than in their hearts and head." We often equate someone's sincerity in the Lord as evidenced by their falling over in fits and shouts and tears.

Booker T. Washington in his book "Up from Slavery' notes that the true sign of repentance was that a person must fall out and remain in a fit like state for some time in order to prove they were sincere. The moaner's bench in the black church represented a place of open repentance and open confession with a tear streaked face. Emotion was the rule of the day.

Now I do believe that we can praise God with our emotions. God made our emotions and we can praise Him with it. He made us to praise Him with our laughter and our tears. He made us even to praise Him with our anger, just don't sin in our anger He admonishes us in Ephesians 4:6.

I don't want the Kenyans to worship like black America worships. Neither do I want them to feel forced to worship like white America.

I was confirmed in the Episcopalian church, before I was baptized and ordained a Deacon in the Baptist church. I found a great deal of joy in the quietness and awe of the Episcopalian church. I was raised singing Gregorian chants in the Anglican church choir before I learned to moan and harmonize in the male chorus at New Hope Baptist. I find a great deal of comfort in the incense and candles and robes and the quiet of the cathedral because they point to the awe and mystery of God.

This God I learned about is a God I can become friends with, but He's not just one of the guys on the block. Jesus is my friend, He is my pal. But Jesus is my Christ. I cannot approach this Christ in anyway. I must approach Him with awe.

That however, does not require a policeman to tell me how to do this. What these police fail to recognize is that my relationship with God cannot be monitored the whole time. There is a long highway and though I may obey the rules while they have the speed traps, in my heart I know they won't always be around.

We have given people a vehicle to know Jesus as Lord. We have shown them that worshiping this unknown god, or the god of their ancestors is not the way to eternal life. However, we must not let them fall in love with the vehicle.

They must not assume the vehicle is their new God. The vehicle is only the means to get to the destination. As they keep their eyes on the destination the vehicle loses its appeal. If we monitor people's dreams, they will be afraid to imagine.

If they cannot imagine, they can never invent. If they can never invent, they will never move beyond the things we give them. We cannot dream their dreams for them.

The Bible is the word of God. However, even the Bible reveals there are somethings still unknown. Isaiah states there are things which remain unrevealed to the heart, mind of man in Isaiah 64:4. This is reiterated in 1 Cor 2:9 Eye hath not seen, nor ear heard, neither have entered into the heart of man, the things which God hath prepared for them that love him again in Isaiah 64:4 these words are found It would appear to me that there are things which even the vehicle which we use to know God has revealed there are things which are yet kept secret to God '....even so the things of God knoweth no man, but the Spirit of God' 1 Cor 2:16 and.

We must be careful not to the people we serve in an effort to make them praise God as we do. We may become their models, the vehicle by which they come know God. We want to be sure that they do not get stuck riding the vehicle, admiring the vehicle and forget the destination Jesus. We must decrease so He can increase.

HOW MANY MONKEYS
DOES IT TAKE TO FIX A WATCH?

I toured the Kenya National museum in Nairobi and I was upset. I saw the exhibition of evolution with the depiction of man's earliest beginnings in Africa. According to Leakey's model in the museum, the ape in Africa came to be a man. If we follow this argument to its logical or illogical conclusion, the African is closest to the ape. I saw this same illustration in one of the Kenyan school textbooks and I began to recognize just how damaging this evolutionary lie was to the African psyche. Africans were being taught that man descended from the ape in Africa. This was part of school curriculum. Whatever happened to being made in the divine image of God? This is truly brainwashing in the name of science. It has hurt Kenyans in my opinion as I recognize it hurt African Americans also.

'How many monkeys does it take to fix this watch?' is my attempt to take a look at some of the ongoing discrepancies of life in Africa as seen from the African American perspective. The title actually comes from some rhetoric I heard while in surgery training in Philadelphia. The attending surgeons were known to do everything to discourage you from learning if they were not particularly fond of you.

They would look in the operating room I was in and refer to me with such disparaging things as 'He may not be good, but he sure is slow....., and..., he is ambidextrous, he can't do anything with either hand..., and..., it looks like three monkeys in there trying to fix a watch!' One attending in particular would look at me and recite his version of the United Negro College Fund slogan and state; 'What a waste!'

Now I look back and realize their intention was that I never develop the confidence to be what God wanted me to be. I knew they meant me no good, but I never realized the extent of their intention. When I went to Africa, I began to see for the first time, just how much discouragement can effect a culture as it had deeply effected me. I was always looking over my shoulder to see if I could get approval by the attending physician, who happened to be a white man. I could not look for such encouragement in people of my own kith and kindred as they had no power to grant the degree, nor the certification.

My academic questions were not of the kind; 'what are the implications of this treatment versus its alternative' but rather, 'can I make this good enough not to be laughed at, or do I need to call in another monkey?'

In retrospect, this undermining of my confidence began a lot earlier than that. I can recall instances throughout my childhood now which seemed rather normal to me, because I was already convinced that white people were intellectually superior. I never questioned it when my white high school counselors would tell me that I was not smart enough to make it into medical school, because obviously they knew best.

When I went out for track as a senior in high school, my white track coach reminded me that 'black people don't do well in long distance running', so it was best that I stick with short sprints. I dare not relate this story to my Kenyan friends, whose nation now produces the best long distance runners in history.

I remember how black men were 'not smart enough' to play baseball, quarterback a football team, nor 'agile enough' to play basketball. When I was growing up in the mid 1950's to early 1960's, there were at best two black men on any NBA team. The insidious lies that we were not sophisticated enough to play golf or tennis have slowly give way to truth as black Americans have excelled and broken records in each of these sporting events. However, when I was growing up, I was still comparing myself to the monkey.

At the University of Michigan Medical School, one instructor of physiology would stand in the front of the classroom and proclaim how the less developed races had a different metabolism and hence were genetically inferior. I could not sit through this drivel and my refusal to listen to this shut out a lot of the other more important things he said.

After my third year in Africa, I began to notice that I didn't need to look for monkeys to help me out. I began to notice that if I could avoid looking for monkeys, I could find the solutions in myself, as God had given me sound reasoning and ability. However, I could now face other people, Kenyans in particular, and see that they were looking for monkeys and I could help them out of this unnecessary search.

We were celebrating our wedding anniversary. We decided we would go to one of the nicer vacation spots since our status as residents in the country afforded us discounts of about one third of the usual price. It was the Lake Naivasha country club. A very pleasant place with a variety of tropical birds flitting around its well manicured lawns. The grass was so green as to make you think it was artificial. At night, you could hear the hippos grunt and on occasion, one would come up on the grass near the cabins in which we slept. It is truly a beautiful place.

Of course, it is mostly frequented by tourists and white tourist at that. We were not surprised because, they have a lot more money.

As we strolled through the lobby, we walked by a table of white tourists who were sipping on fruit punch and sodas. One Kenyan, a black man was amongst them and he was laughing at the jokes they shared and they all appeared to be having a good time. Then this man decided to make a good joke. He began to tell how much he disliked Americans of African decent. "You know they don't really speak English very well. They have a very crude accent. They slur their words and use dis.., and dat..., and whodat..., and I don't respect them because they are so poorly educated"

The white visitors seemed a bit annoyed at what he was saying and only chuckled a bit. No one seemed to feel it was politically appropriate to demean their fellow citizens. They were confused. It was obvious that even they knew that monkeys don't fix watches.

However, this man did not perceive his failings and persisted with a few more lines of mocking black American diction.

I looked around and noticed that Kay had disappeared before this act had started. I was..., upset. I didn't know whether to hit the man or spit on him. I was afraid if I spat on him, it might get on the other guests and I knew hitting him would not get the results I wanted and he might beat me up.

I walked over to him in the middle of his chuckling and politely asked him; "Would you kindly repeat, just what it is you don't like about us?"

There was a hush over the entire gathering. The white guests who were his audience now looked at the comedian and then at me. The comedian's eyes got wide and his mouth stood open. I could almost hear his heart beat as he gulped air. I think he was trying to gather back the words he had spoken.

He finally spoke; "Aaa..whaa, whaa..., what did you say?"

I repeated myself; "I just want to know what it is about black Americans you find so offensive."

He had no answer for me as he searched his minds for the monkeys to fix his watch and his white guests sat stupefied and mute. I had just brought down the curtain on this act.

A few minutes later he came to me apologizing. "I didn't mean anything by what I was saying. Will you forgive me?"

I was too angry to discuss it further and decided it would be best to get away from this man before I did something which would get us both in trouble. But more importantly, I saw in this man the same struggle I had in my own life. I saw the continuing need to beat the slave out of myself as much as I wanted to beat it out of him.

How could I condemn this man who was only trying to impress these white tourists so they would give him a bigger tip and recommend him for other tour operators? Even I know that the easiest way to get a big tip from white people is to make them smile and laugh. It has been a part of our culture for a long time. When a black man is smiling, he is usually not dangerous. This is why in America we have many more black comics than news commentators. He needed to act like a fool in order to impress white people..., or so he thought. He needed to show them that monkeys may not be able to fix a watch, but they sure can be fools.

A GOOD EXAMPLE

I did not mean to offend anyone in the room. In my anger and frustration I pleaded to the staff in the middle of the case; 'Why can't we get these things done on time? We have had at least one hundred cases like this within this year. Why does it seem like it is the first time every time we do it? Can't we get the instruments prepared before the case?'

A hush fell over the operating room. My coworker Kenyans looked at me in awe. They had gotten used to my arrogance. They did not like it, but they seemed to say; 'Let's just let him blow off steam and we can get right back to the way things always were.'

Some time ago, a few of them related to me that they would only get serious about their work when a missionary would happen by. I know this feeling from my own culture in America. We would say things like 'Watch out! Here comes the man!' or, 'Here comes Mister Charlie.' This was in reference to the white man who owned, oversaw or managed the place of our employment. I knew just what they were feeling.

We had come a long way in improving the quality of care in the operating room. However, I did not want things to get back to the way they always were. This was precisely the point I was trying to make. How could I get these guys to realize that the inefficiency in the operating room led to patients remaining in the hospital for longer periods of time? The spinal anesthesia was already given and this patient was not going to have the surgery because they did not prepare the instruments. We were endangering this man's life and health and adding to the cost of his stay, all because someone did not prepare the instruments the night before.

I had looked at the x-rays, lab reports, talked with the patient and family and read the book on the surgery I was to perform. I had done my part. Why couldn't they do their part? Why did they all stand there staring at me with a smile as if to say; 'What's the big deal?'

I thought I would try another approach. Something which would allow me to identify with them as a Christian brother and a son of Africa. I felt a little shock therapy would help.

"You know", I started off in my best Swahili "they tell me that Africans are stupid and lazy. They tell me that Africans are not good workers only followers. This really hurts me because I am a son of Africa and I don't want to feel that about my people." Then I paused and sweated. It was quite a risk I was taking. I was gambling that my African camouflage would allow me some license here.

I was sure they would get the message now. They could definitely read between the lines and see that I wanted to identify with them and encourage them to follow a shining example of working with an ethic that reflected their love of Jesus. After all, why was I here, but to reflect the love of Jesus? Although it more often appeared to be the wrath of the devil.

The room remained silent. Everyone looked to his fellow worker and smiled and snickered.

I see now that I had proved my point. I had been able to win them over to the kind of thinking that would reflect the glory of God. And just to add a final punch, I put one more question to them.

"Now if we are to reflect the love of God in our work, what example should we follow?" I knew for certain the message was clear and distinct now as every forehead was filled with furrows reflecting deep reflection and quiet meditation. But in keeping with tradition, no one dare speak before the most senior person in the room had spoken. I looked towards, lets call him Dwight. I knew Dwight would have an answer. Dwight was the only formally trained staff person in the room, having completed nursing school.

Dwight had shown some deep spiritual insight during our morning devotions in the operating room. Dwight was a man of 40 plus years in age and was a faithful father and husband. Dwight was the head of the operating room staff and made the schedules for all of the crew. Dwight oversaw the orders and inventories of the supplies. Dwight administered anesthesia and monitored the patients during the procedures. I knew I could trust Dwight.

We all waited and looked towards Dwight. Dwight smiled, revealing the absent two middle bottom teeth which some of his tribe remove in order to prove their manhood. It was a joyous smile, like a kid who had just found a treasure. He smiled and said; 'Dr. Johnson I know how we should do our work. We should do our work, just like the white man!'

Everyone in the room groaned and laughed nervously as I shouted.... "NO! NO! NO!. We are to do our work as unto the

Lord!"   It was obvious to me now that even Dwight would look for a monkey to fix his watch.

I have been blessed to have worked in the nation of Kenya for many years now. I have met some of the most keen intellects and men of great integrity within the nation of Kenya, black Kenyan, men and women who are an inspiration to anyone who meets them. Some of these people work in government and some are in private business. Some of these men and women are teachers, preachers and some are farmers and common laborers.

I have been blessed to have them share with me their lives and their stories about life. They have wrestled with this same misperception and misrepresentation of their culture and traditions. They are well aware that monkeys don't fix watches.

MY BEAUTY IS MY BEAST

I thought I could hear the bones in her back creak. After all, the load she carried was at least one and one half times her weight. It was a cupboard, the size of a small pantry. The doors were tied shut and the drawers were all locked so as not to open as she stumbled over the rocks and ruts on the side of the road. The tall grass and weeds hid all of the small pebbles and biting insects which distracted her as she tried to balance this piece of furniture on her back. It would have been easier to walk in the paved road, except then she would have to dodge the fast moving vehicles like mine and balance her cargo.

Her husband was several paces in front of her. It was raining and he seemed a bit annoyed at getting wet. As he carried his walking cane, he would on occasion pause in his stride to make sure his wife was making some headway along the route. He did not want this precious piece damaged in any way and if it were, she would surely deserve a beating when she got home.

As we sped by in our diesel powered, turbo charged Land Rover, we slowed to survey this scene more closely. It was typical in Kenya. I had seen mothers recover from ceseran-sections for the delivery of twins, pack the two infants on their backs, bundle their belongings in a suitcase and leave the hospital with all of these things to carry as their proud husbands walked ahead a distance so as not to be tempted to help them should they stumble and fall. Callous? Perhaps. But this is tradition in many parts of Kenya. Why should a man do a woman's work?

My Kenyan friends in the car wondered why I was slowing down to observe this woman carrying the cupboard in the rain. "What is wrong with that Michael? You think the husband should carry that burden," one of them asked?

I replied; "I do think it would help them to get home quicker if they would share the load."

The proudest one of the group, let's call him George, then spoke up. "You see, Michael, your problem is you don't look at this as we do. Our Kenyan women are proud to carry a load like this. I have seen your American women there at Tenwek go jogging in the day. They do this to stay in shape. Our women don't have to jog. They don't need those fancy aerobic machines and exercises. They get their exercise by working!"

If I had thought of this story myself, I would never have imagined anyone could really be that stupid. Did he really believe this? Was he trying to tell me he was really proud of the way this man was treating his wife? Was he going to treat his own wife this way? Was the wife a beast of burden or a bride of beauty? I have been told by many men that they indeed choose their wives based upon the strength of their biceps and the workload they can tolerate. Life can be rough in the country and a mate who can pull her load is a whole lot better than one who just looks good.

Beauty is only skin deep when it comes to fetching water, wood, weeding the garden and starting fires for the evening. Why marry a Hollywood model who is afraid of breaking a fingernail, when you need a woman who can carry the furniture on her back?

But is this something to be proud of? Couldn't this man afford a mule to carry this burden? Why not a cart pulled by two mules so he and his wife could ride? Why must this Kenyan friend of mine feel it logical to defend this treatment of this man's soul mate?

I looked over at George and asked him; "If you really think this is better than aerobic exercises, why is it that Kenyan women live shorter lives? How does a man expect a woman after spending ten to twelve hours of this kind of labor, to give him any tender intimacy when he gets home? How does a man expect his wife to respect him as a person, when he treats her as a beast?"

These were rhetorical questions I know because, George looked at me as though I was asking him 'how many monkeys does it take to fix a watch?'

My point in these stories is that we as black people on both sides of the ocean and around the world have been made to feel inferior. We are the only ones who can put a stop to this nonsense. We are not inferior beings who evolved from apes as depicted in the books which teach evolution as a science.

We are not descendants of animals. We are created in the image of God as we are told in Genesis and as we accept Christ, God's son as our salvation, we will be remade, born again in His image. As sons of God, as joint heirs in Christ, we will recognize we can indeed accomplish great things for God. Indeed we are promised in Philippians 4:13 that we can do all things through Christ who strengthens us.

DON'T SHOP WITH
WHITE PEOPLE. IT'S NO FUN!

This may sound like a cruel statement, but I stand by it nonetheless. As I have stated earlier, it is good to be with white people when you are in Africa, most of the time. There is protection because it is dangerous to kill a white person. There is prestige, because no matter where you go, you will for the most part be let in the front of the line and do not have to worry about being turned away. If you want to get ahead as a black man in Africa, go with somebody white. Except for shopping.

White people will never get a bargain shopping. No one believes there are any white people who don't have money in Kenya. I am bound to say that I am prejudiced to this degree as well. If I ever see a white person hitch hiking in Kenya the thought that comes to my mind is; "This is a some deranged person. If I give them a ride, I will probably have to give them the car too."

Hence, if even someone of my high intellect (don't snicker) can feel this way, what must those of less exposure to the ways of the world think?

I make it a point to hide myself in the crowd when I go shopping. It's easy as I have been born with African camouflage. In addition, both Kay and I have learned Swahili to the point that many Kenyans say we speak it better than they. It comes in handy in the market place. We bicker and bargain in the national language and remain undetected as counterfeit Kenyans.

It is in the market place where you try not to meet your white friends. The price on everything will at least triple once they see the white of their skin. Well for that matter, even our Japanese and Korean friends have the same problem. Everyone assumes they are wealthy.

Of course by Kenyan standards, practically all people of the non-African hue are enormously wealthy. This is the reason you don't see unemployed white people in Kenya. (Some of the missionaries feel the salary looks like unemployment benefits).

Any white, or Asian (as they call those whose origin is from India) person who wants a job could find some Kenyan to employ him. Just try this experiment.

Walk into any store in Kenya. If you see a black Kenyan and a non -black person behind the counter, what is your impression of who is in charge? 99.9 percent of the time, you will assume the non-black person is in charge. In this sense, a white person can lend legitimacy to many enterprises in Kenya just by being at the front desk or front door (except as bellboy, and then don't call him boy).

Kenyans tell me that in Nairobi even up to the time of liberation in 1963, they were not allowed on certain streets and in certain communities. To do so could mean imprisonment, punishment and under the right circumstances death if one did not have a pass or permission to be in an all white area. The Nairobi Club and other establishments and hospitals were off limits to black Kenyans and even Indians (Asians as they are called). The Nairobi Hospital was first known as the European Hospital and only later added wards for Asians and finally native born black Africans.

Wealth was something Africans were never meant to acquire in this country. They were supposed to remain on the fringes of society and serve those who were really in power. They were never meant to be rich.

I never considered myself as rich until I went to Kenya. At one point when the drought was at its worse, we took a trip to some of the more arid regions of the country. These areas were hit very hard by the drought. As we rode in our car, we saw dozens of dead carcasses of cattle along the roads and in the fields. The nomadic people who once owned these animals were moving with what remained of their herds. The animals which had thus far survived were literally skin and bones.

There was not enough flesh on them to sell at any market so moving the herd was the only option. There was no grass, no water, only more desert and more sand. As I watched these people move by in a silent sad stream I noticed the things they carried. A train of donkeys was laden with their few belongings. Some bits and pieces of leather used for making shields and shoes, some tools and remnants of furniture from their homes. The people themselves looked tired and desperate. Nothing but dust and despair.

I knew how rich I was then. I carried more things to the bathroom in the morning than these people had for their livelihood. I go to the bathroom with a bathrobe, slippers, shaving kit, toothbrush, dental floss, a loofa, soap on a rope, back brush and a pumice stone to scrape my feet. a change of clothes and a clean towel and face rag. I usually take something to read as I might be there a while and of course my reading glasses (not enough fiber in the diet). If I feel real industrious, I will take my manicure and pedicure set along with something to remove my nose hairs (hair grows in different places when you get older). I really am rich. They would never believe otherwise should I want to buy some of their leather works or other arts and crafts.

I recognized that in my fifteen-foot trek to the bathroom, I was going to flush down the toilet more and better water than they would see in a month. In fact for their daily trek of 20 miles or so, the only thing they would drink would be cow's milk, mixed with cow blood.

The approach when interviewing one of these people to determine if they have a bladder infection, one question is how often do you urinate? When you consider that they only take in a miniscule amount of fluids, the answer of 'once daily' is understandable. I have given up asking; "How often do you bathe"

These people were never supposed to get rich. They were supposed to stay in the back woods and never become a part of the system. When the schools were made for them, they could at best be to train them to be workers, but never thinkers.

As a black American I saw so many similarities in the system. Our schools of higher learning were originally designed to teach us a trade, a vocation because we were not supposed to be able to think. Just witness the nationwide debate over the funding of public school education in the inner cities versus vouchers. Separate but equal always has been separate, but never equal. We had separate colleges, known early on as industrial colleges as opposed to liberal arts or universities.

We were supposed to remain on the edge of respectability. We were not supposed to excel in anything to make us wealthy. This is still an attitude which is present today. We have not completely done away with our traditions of keeping some people poor and ignorant for the sake of profit in America. The newspapers of America are frequently filled with reports of the struggle between providing necessary schools for the inner city versus the new stadiums.

Educating the residents of the cities is not a priority. A survey of schools in Philadelphia by the Inquirer newspaper (Public School Report Card 1998-99; Philadelphia Inquirer) shows a distinct disparity of spending in school districts dominated by people of color. The total dollars spent per student per year showed disparities as high as 20 percent less spending in economically disadvantaged areas. In addition the teachers in these areas were holding fewer higher degrees and had a pay differential of 15-20 percent than those in more economically advantaged areas.

However, many initiatives for building stadiums and other places of amusement within those same disadvantaged population centers is a nationwide trend of dubious benefit to those same people as concluded by the Heartland Institutes report.

The Heartland Institute is a nonprofit research and education organization based in Chicago, Illinois. This paper is based on comments he made to the Indianapolis Economic Forum on October 1,1997

Spending money to educate people of color has never been a priority in the US nor in Africa. In Africa and Europe author

Norman Bennet notes that 'in 1951 only one individual out of the 16,000,000 indigenous inhabitants of Northern Nigeria possessed a university degree.' He notes further that 'Opportunities for Africans in higher education were extremely limited until very late in the colonial period.' To date, not a single head of state, i.e. President, of Nigeria has had a college degree.

My son Elijah was sitting at a restaurant near his school recently, quietly eating breakfast and reading the newspaper. He overheard two middle-aged white men comment; 'He must be one of those intellectual ones...., I bet he really can't even read that paper.' Elijah chose to ignore them, though I know he was hurt. He told me he did not want to expend too much energy on this encounter as he had to take the medical school admissions test later that day. He was defying the legacy they thought he should follow.

Kenyans were only allowed to go to school to learn trades which use their hands. The schools were deliberately designed to limit their abilities to think or act independently. Thus, their abilities to earn money were severely limited. If you were black in Kenya and wanted to achieve, you must have a white sponsor.

Whites and Asians were on different tracks in school as well. Asians took courses designed to make them the overseer of black labor and whites were by virtue of their color deemed the bosses. Hence, the stain remains on the brain of Kenyans that there are no poor, nor ignorant white people, only poor and ignorant black people.

When the British granted independence, it has been said they gave the Indians the businesses, they themselves kept the banks and allowed the Kenyans to have the government. Kenyans had the reigns of government, without the resources to govern.

My friend and co-worker Sam Powdrill illustrates it like this. He went to rescue his Mahindra car which was broken down in the 'bush' areas of Kenya. Sam drove his Land Cruiser which is almost a locomotive on rubber wheels, and he pushed the Mahindra back home. The Mahindra is a vehicle, which in my estimation, should be reserved for use as a golf cart. Sam did not want to wear out the brakes of the Mahindra pulling it behind him with a tow rope, so he pushed it instead. His Kenyan worker was steering the Mahindra as Sam pushed him from behind.

Now the only one who can see the potholes, and pitfalls in the road is the man in the Mahindra, with the motor which does not start, hence no horn, no lights, or windshield wipers to clean off the mud hindering his view of inanimate objects like trees and stones or those obstacles petrified with terror, like galloping goats, slow moving cattle and of course little children. The Mahindra man is moving forward only because the driver in the locomotive wants it so. He cannot relate the potential tragedies ahead and has to depend upon the man behind him to see things through two dirty windshields. He makes no decisions as to what direction, or speed he travels.

This somewhat illustrates what happens in African governments as well as mission work in many instances. The Kenyans hold the reigns of government, but the true power is driven by 'global' companies who harvest the fruit, the tea, coffee and provide the tourists with safe places for vacations. It reinforces the sense of not being either incapable, or incompetent to control one's own destiny. The driving force must come from whites.

Almost any white missionary who visits the most remote regions of Kenya will be considered to have a great degree of knowledge. They will at least be considered to be able to treat and heal with modern western medicines, even if they have no degree in science, medicine or related fields. We assume a lot about people based upon color.

When purchasing our house in Upper Darby Pennsylvania in 1980, the realtors did not want to show it to us as they knew we could not afford it. They had no idea of my profession or income, they only looked at my skin color to determine I was not worthy of such a fine house in such a fine neighborhood.

It is really the same for all of America for that matter. Go to any small store in America with any mix of people of a variety of skin colors and hues. Take a look at any large financial firm or business enterprise with the same mix. You will most likely assume those of lighter hue are in charge, especially if it is a white man rather than a white woman. The joke amongst black people is that we don't believe it until 'it comes from the mouth of a white man'.

That is why I don't shop with white people. Just when you get the vendor down to a good price, up walks missionary John Smith. He starts talking to you and you try to ignore him.

I pretend I don't speak English. But somehow, John doesn't get the message. I want to scream; "Ixnay on the Englishay John!" But he doesn't get it. My eyes don't relay the message in time.

Hi Mike! How are things at the hospital?" John is in a bubbly mood.

"Oh the work is just as usual John". I raise my voice a bit now. "We are hoping for SOME MORE AMERICANS LIKE YOU to come over and help." This is the best I can do to throw the vendor a curve ball. It doesn't work. I've been spotted as an African wannabe.

The price of the cabbage Kay has chosen just went from the equivalent of 20 U.S. cents to 50 US cents. Now she will only buy one. Well, I am in one sense glad. I have less to carry as her houseboy. Maybe shopping with white folks around does have some advantages.

AM I MY BROTHER'S KEEPER?

THE SEARCH FOR AN AFRICAN AMERICAN IDENTITY IN MISSIONS

Genesis 4 gives an account of the first murder. We can see clearly the motive of Cain to kill Abel. God had taken greater delight in the gift of Abel. Cain killed Abel because he was jealous of him. The Biblical record says that God asked Cain of his brother's whereabouts. Cain replied; "I know not: Am I my brother's keeper?"

It is with this rhetorical question we address God when we ask is it our responsibility to do world missions. Whose job is it to evangelize the world? Whose job is it to feed the hungry, clothe the naked, and visit the sick and imprisoned? Whose job is it to encourage the downcast? Whose job is it to minister to the materially rich but spiritually impoverished?

This is the real question in missions. This is the question each of us is really asking God when we consider whether we are called and to where we are called. It is not the question of "Should I go to Africa, Asia, Europe or South America?" The question really is "Am I my brother's keeper?"

Now this is not the first time God has heard this question as you will recall. Abel was dead and hidden in the sand having been killed by his brother Cain. God was asking for some account-ability and Cain tried to play a mind game on the Creator of the mind. "Who do you think you are..., God or somebody like that? Aren't you supposed to be in charge? If you know everything, why are you asking me where this guy Abel is? You find him! He is not in my charge..., I am not his keeper!"

Who do you think you are...,God? I just got a new job and I finally got enough money to get cable television. I finally made it into a class of people which will allow me the prestige of owning a home. I just got a position which allows me to wear a tie and dress well. I just paid off my student loans. I finally got the kind of car I want and the kind of jewelry everyone else has. What has that trouble over there got to do with me over here? Don't I have enough trouble with my own people here? Let them folk take care of their own. I am not my brother's keeper.

After all those people don't even look like me. They believe different things. They have different traditions. What right do I have imposing my religion and my beliefs on them. I know this Jesus stuff is okay for me and my traditions, just let those folks be over there. I may call Him King of kings and Lord of lords, but I only meant that He is so around here. Those folk have their own beliefs.

Why are African Americans in missions so few in numbers? Have we abandoned the call? Do we not read the same Gospel? Do we not share the same burden? Do we not identify with the downtrodden and outcast of the world? Are we not able to meet the call? Are we not prepared? Do we not have the resources? When we answer all of these questions we are still faced with the original query posed by Cain: "Am I my brother's keeper?"

Missionary activity has always had a mixed agenda. Early missionaries from Europe to Africa and the Americas were frequently used by the colonial governments to soften up the natives in order to make them more accepting of economic conquest. European governments ravaged Africa in the name of Christ. Early American missionaries to the native Americans the so-called Indians, were at times used as an experiment by the US government to make the Indians passive. They even taught the Indians how to buy and use slaves for labor.

Missionary activity in Africa was almost exclusively a European phenomenon, part and parcel of its colonial conquests. America itself had no colonies in Africa. However, it sought to establish such in the early 1800's. The American Colonization Society was founded in 1816 with the intent by the administration of President James Monroe, of establishing a colony in Liberia. The United States used former slaves as Christian missionaries to establish a presence in Africa.

This was with the duel intent of ridding the US of freedmen or former slaves who were deemed a threat in the southern states to the institution of slavery and establishing a US presence in Africa. Freed slaves were also seen as a menace in the northern states because they had the effrontery to expect to be treated as equals in society.

The propagation of the Gospel was not infrequently a side issue when we consider the history of mission activities of Europe and America in the 19th and 20th centuries. Economic, cultural and military domination have been part and parcel of the package of benefits given to evangelized masses.

The fact that the church is established in many parts of the world for profit is not a new phenomenon. Paul noted in Philippians 1:15-18; "Some indeed preach Christ even of envy and strife and some also of good will..., What then? Notwithstanding every way, Whether it is pretence or in truth, Christ is preached." The church is established in spite of missionary efforts in many instances.

Because of this very mixed history, and perceptions (whether real or imagined) of good and bad in missions, many of us have avoided the calling to serve God in this capacity. I myself recall the feelings of revulsion which swept over me when I considered going to work as an overseas missionary. I found myself recalling the horror stories I had heard. White men and women going to Africa and Asia and setting up for themselves little kingdoms in Jesus' name. I heard that these people even to this day continued to exploit people of color in order to live a good life in a kind of postcolonial era, having all of the good parts of the land.

I recalled pictures of Africans carrying heavy loads on their heads sweating in the hot humid mosquito filled, malaria jungles. These African 'brutes' carried pianos in the hot, humid, snake infested jungles so the 'civilized' Christian missionary could enjoy teaching them to sing 'Jesus loves me' while the 'dumb' African cooked in the hut outside their home. The missionary I saw in my mind was an older white man wearing a pit helmet, being carried on a cot or chair, lifted by four sweaty black men, all smiling despite the pain of carrying this 'black man's burden' and singing 'glory, glory, glory'.

This picture was revolting to my every sensibility. How could I possibly associate myself with such a group of people? How could I stoop so low as to associate myself with a culture known for its exploitation of every culture it had encountered? How could I even identify myself with knowing the same God as they did? In fact, did we know the same God?

How could I justify being a missionary? Is there any precedent for missions within my own people? Are there any people of color of whom it can be said they are missionaries?

These questions troubled me as I am sure they trouble anyone of African ancestry. We need to consider this call of carrying the Gospel of Christ to all nations. Christ has indeed been preached by many people for many reasons. Nonetheless, Christ has been preached. I can say this much in defense of my white brothers and sisters. If they had never gone, many people of the world today would have no schools, no hospitals and no development. Many of our white brothers and sisters have sacrificed their health, careers, fortune and their lives in bringing Jesus to the nations.

How do we find our place in this calling of missions? Do we have a history and a place of reference? Well to be sure, some of the earliest, if not first American missionaries were of African descent. George Leile immigrated to Jamaica in 1782 in order to carry the gospel of Christ after buying his freedom from his white slave masters.

African Americans have been at the forefront of missions even before the American Colonization Society to Liberia. This calling continued and was sustained in such agencies as the Union Missionary Society formed by the freed man James Pennington in 1841, which sent African American missionaries to Sierra Leone.

In 1864 the first African American likened physician and surgeon in the state of Tennessee, Georgia E. Patton Washington, was also one of the first African American medical missionary in Africa. History also tells us of Lott Cary, who was born into slavery and became a well to do Baptist preacher in Richmond Virginia. However, he was called to Liberia to function both clergyman and physician in the early 19th century. The Lott Cary foreign mission board is still active today as are several other predominant African American mission agencies. They lack most importantly, missionaries who are willing to go.

In the late 19th and early to mid 20th centuries African Americans were frequently hampered in their calling to missions because white agencies were fearful of them. Mary McLeod Bethune studied at the prodigious Moody Bible Institute of Chicago and applied to be a missionary in Africa. However, she was refused by white agencies who did not want African Americans. Montrose Waite was likewise first accepted and worked with the

Christian Missionary Alliance. He was later rejected as a missionary with this organization because of his color.

Black missionary experience has not been limited to nations of Africa or nations of the African Diaspora as demonstrated in the work of Betsy Stockton. Betsy was born into slavery as property of Robert Stockton. He later presented her as a wedding gift to his daughter. She was eventually freed and after enrollment at Princeton Theological Seminary, she accompanied her former owners, the Stewart family, to Hawaii, where she served as the first African American missionary to the islands helping in education. She learned the Hawaiian languages and taught diverse subjects, including English, Latin, algebra and history.

White mission boards were fearful that colonial governments during these early years might reject their agencies because free and outspoken people of color would undermine their economic interests. Furthermore, 'conservative' boards were still uncomfortable allowing mixing of the races especially when this might result in people of color assuming administrative roles. When I first started writing this book, my family represented the only people of African origin in our agency's then 80 plus year history. This is changing today, as the leadership recognizes the need to be more representative of the world to whom they are sent to serve.

All of these facts notwithstanding, where do we fit in as a people. Is it our calling? Are we our brother's keeper? Do we have a role in missions, or is it the responsibility of our white cohorts in Christ

It is often argued that indeed we are our brother's keeper, but the problems are so big at home to even begin thinking about support overseas. A woman recently approached me and said, "Dr. Johnson, as soon as I hit the lottery, I am going to send you a big donation." I have been told by others that I need to approach the millionaires in our society, the rich black people for support. I think by this they mean the Michael Jordans and Oprah Winfreys of the world.

This is amazing that Christians think that people who never profess a knowledge of Christ should support the work of evangelizing the world for Christ. Is it their job to do this work? Whose calling is this? Shouldn't the Christian to whom the Bible is written, be responsible for advancing the cause of Christ?

Whose job is it to support missionaries? We somehow have the mistaken notion that we must have a million dollars to perform the work. Quite frankly, of the $4,500 per month we raise for our support, the majority comes in $10 per month and $20 per month shares. The average black American church with 200 members or so could easily support our work if each member gave just $22 per month. That amounts to about seventy cents per day, or the amount we spend on cigarettes (I know you personally don't smoke), sodas, cable television and other essentials of life.

Jesus was very clear on this subject of big gifts. He made it clear that the widow's mite was sufficient when given with a spirit of love Mark 12:42. The God whom we serve was able to take the little boy's fish and bread and make a meal to feed thousands John 6:9. Why are we hoarding the little bit we have? Why is it important for us to collect so many things of this world? Don't we recognize Paul's admonition that we are becoming dung collectors (Philippians 3:8)? We are storing up things in this life and not being rich towards God (Luke 12:21). We are building a legacy within our homes for our children to observe and to follow.

We show our children that we only give to God's work when it is convenient and not when it is inconvenient. We show God to be a God who only requires us to give when we have everything in our home. We show our children and the world that unless our God has blessed us in the manner we feel is comfortable, we need not worry about giving to missions. We are only our brother's keeper if God gives us enough. Otherwise it is the rich man's responsibility. It is the government's job. We can always just pray and let God do the work. Unless God gives me more, I am not my brother's keeper.

I know this desire for more of the world. I wrestle with this desire for more. As a boy growing up in America, I wanted for so long to know if we were the poor people. I had heard that black people were poor. It was somehow apparent to me that I was indeed black. I knew that having more was part of the American way of life. I learned this on television and radio. I saw it in the newspapers. Everyone wanted more. Everyone deserved more. Everyone could have more if they just worked long enough and hard enough.

I bought into this American dream of having more. I felt that if I studied hard and long in school I could achieve this American dream. Unfortunately, or fortunately I was later to learn that it takes more than just hard work, it takes a whole lot of grace when you are of a darker hue in this nation.

God provided for me sufficient grace in the form of a godly mother and grandmother and aunt. They taught me more about the importance of giving than the obsession of getting. My mother showed me the importance of living a life that reflected God. That reflection of God she showed me was a God who gave His best to people, not because they deserved the best but because He was able to give the best. I learned very early on that getting and having is temporary and deadly, but giving and sharing is eternal and life giving.

We never get what we deserve. Cain did not get what he deserved when he killed his brother and arrogantly approached God with the question; "Am I my brother's keeper?" It was as though he was saying to God; "Why didn't you keep an eye on him God, after all, if you had protected him, he would be alright!" My mother and my grandmother taught me that I needed to be responsible for the poor and helpless.

I learned very early on that I was my brother's keeper as I listened to Dr. Martin Luther King expound upon the issues of not just black America, but a world that was caught up in corruption and war and hate and civil unrest. Dr. King brought the Viet-Nam conflict to the forefront of black America thought when we were more settled in wrestling with the racism we faced in our own lives and made us see that oppression anywhere in the world is just the same as oppression on our front door step. I learned from Dr. King that I am my brother's keeper.

I have often had to be reminded of my calling to my brother. As I went through school in the '60's, 70's and 80's, it was indeed a long time. Lawrence University in Wisconsin, University of Michigan Medical School and Graduate Hospital in Philadelphia for training in surgery, I often forgot about my brother.

As I finished training in surgery in Philadelphia, I shut out the horrors of the world around me and began to focus on me, myself and I. What did I want in life? What did I need in life? After all, don't I deserve more? I've been poor for so long!

That is our theme song as a people today. Don't we deserve more? Of course we do. Cain did not get all he deserved either, did he? What more did Cain deserve? Cain deserved hell. What more do we deserve? We deserve hell. But God who is rich in mercy for His great love for which He loved us, even when we were dead in our sins, hath quickened us together with Christ. Ephesians 2:4-5. God did not give us what we deserve, He gave us His only Son as the only way to eternal life.

But Lord, we have been poor for so long. We've been down for so long Lord. Don't you see our sad estate? Lord give us more! We prayed for more. We prayed for freedom from slavery. We prayed for freedom from the whip of the master and from the vicious reprisal of former slave owners after the Civil War. We prayed for relief from Jim Crow segregation.

We prayed for jobs. We prayed for voting rights. We prayed for fair employment. We prayed for equal representation in government. We prayed for fair courts. We prayed for good schools. These are important things. These are necessary things. We need these things to survive.

We have not gotten all we prayed for or adult friend for something which now you remember would have been harmful. God reminds us in Matthew chapter 7 that God is a good Father who will not give a serpent to us if we ask for a fish. We are told that every good and perfect comes from our Father; James1:17. God wants us to have the best. He would not have us suffer when we would ask for things which are harmful to us. We really don't need nor want all of the things we pray for. It would be like that Chinese curse; " may all of your wishes come true."

We have, by God's grace, not gotten all we pray for. Many of the things we have accomplished in our individual lives are not a result of answered prayer, but of selfish motives and greed. Our homes today are broken by divorce and drugs not as an answer to prayer, but because of our self-reliance.

We have not gotten all we prayed for. However, we have made some gains. We have not and given the present trend of things in America will not get our full share. This does not preclude us from being our brother's keeper.

As I came to the realization that I was given the privileges I had not for self, but to give to others my priorities started to change. Why had all of those people suffered for so long in order for me to get to where I am today? Right now, I admit people to hospitals and operate on those people in the very hospitals that 30 years ago I could not be treated in myself. Why has God given me such a legacy today? Why did He do it? I believe He knew I would wake up one day and remember I am indeed my brother's keeper. God wants us to wake up today and remember that in the midst of all of our struggles, we are our brother's keeper.

Our brother is of course not just in Africa. God has never called us the brotherhood of Africans. This is certainly the worldview. We get sentimental and misty eyed about helping out the poor African brother. We romanticize about the great kings and great empires and great thrones of Africa. We forget of course that in order to have great empires, and great kings sitting on great thrones, there had to be some little people, servants and others, with little gardens sitting in little outhouses.

When it comes to the glories of Africa, we are more interested in the glory of animals than the glory of its people. We watch movies such as Godzilla and National Geographic specials and marvel at the animal life which is guarded against poachers killing, elephants, rhinos and other endangered species, but turn away from the news on CNN or BBC which reveal the massive killing of human life, a less endangered species, with millions of men women and children killed yearly in wars, famines and disasters.

We have made Africa to be a nation of nothing but great things when the Bible is quite clear that there is wickedness in every heart and every corner of the world. Psalm 14:2-3 tells us that God looked down from heaven upon the children of men to see if there were any that did understand and seek God. They are all gone aside, they are all together become filthy; there is none that doeth good, no, not one. Even Africa at its glory was nothing but filthy rags, just as the rest of the world is without Jesus Christ as Savior and Lord.

We are not called just to Africa. We, as members of the body of Christ are called to the world in need of the Savior. We are called not just to the materially impoverished of Angola in Africa, but the spiritually impoverished of Austria in Europe. Our brother is in this sense, anyone who is in need of the Gospel of Christ. God would not give His only Son to accomplish such a limited activity of evangelizing Africa.

So what has God given us to accomplish this great task? He has given us everything we need and quite often everything we asked for. According to the 1996 US census report, there are 34.2 millions black people in America. The median income was for that period $26,520. That means that black workers make approximately in one year what the average Kenyan would make in about 70 years.

In other words, the average black American made in one year what the average Kenyan would make in almost two lifetimes. Not two years, two lifetimes, as the average Kenyan is paid a salary of $300 per year. Compare that $300 per year to $26,520 per year. A recent report from the United Nations reveals that 1.5 billion people live on less than one dollar per day.

Now you might ask; "Is the cost of living cheaper in Kenya?" I would answer, "yes and no." What we consider to be essentials for the cost of living don't figure into the Kenyan economy. There are many people in Kenya who have yet to board a motorized vehicle of any form. There are few homes in Kenya with electricity.

There are few homes with indoor plumbing. There are few families having such luxuries as beds and blankets and pillows. The very idea of eating more than one meal per day is a luxury to many people in Kenya today and very often that meal consists of nothing more than a handful of cornmeal. The newspapers of Kenya for the past few weeks have relate stories of whole communities, families and friends starving to death. Can you imagine what it is like to watch your children starve to death?

So, I ask you; "Is the cost of living cheaper in Kenya?" In a sense it is. That is why life is so short with the life expectancy of Kenyans dropping to below 50 years of age. Living is not cheaper, life is.

Life is cheaper in many parts of the world. So we turn off our cable television because we don't want to see just how cheap it is. As we in Black America boast of the fact that African American owned companies earned over 32 billion dollars in 1992 with spending continuing to spiral we continue to ignore the plight of a world that is facing economic meltdown.

We black Americans boast of spending close to 4 billion dollars on foods and beverages from Black owned companies and continue to disproportionately suffer from obesity, hypertension, diabetes, heart disease and gallstones, diseases which come from eating too much. We don't want to see the pictures of people huddled around a pot of boiled grass and tree leaves in Sudan, trying to feed their starving children.

We flush our toilets with cleaner water than most people of the world are drinking today. We buy $150 dollar sneakers to wear to $5 movie and eat $5 worth of popcorn and candy for a night on the town, while the average family in the world is trying to find a way to make a life for a day in the village.

We spend more on lotteries and casinos as a people, on games of chance, while most women in the world are taking a chance at even getting pregnant as they don't know if they will survive the pregnancy with no doctor in the village.

People in much of the world sit on a dirt floor around an empty table, searching the house for a few coins, watching, waiting, hoping and praying 'Give us this day our daily bread, while we sit around the table with not enough room for the pots and pans of food, won't say a prayer of thanks over supper because we might miss what's on television, as we pray; 'Give us this day our daily number.' As they scratch out a living, we scratch for the daily number.

Farouk Aman is young boy for instance living in southern Sudan. Farouk happens to be a Christian. He is just 17 years old. His chance of living to 30 is very small. For you see, Christian men and women in Southern Sudan are being chased on foot for hundreds of miles and executed by having their throats slit open by their enemies

Their children are running into the hills to escape their captors and yet are being sold into slavery today, while we in Black America boast that our black owned car dealers sell over 6 billion dollars per year of products we don't even produce.

We would not walk the distance to work that these people are forced to run for their lives, yet we continue to try to buy the finest autos and ride in the latest style because we want to keep up with the "Joneses".

God has given us all that we need to meet the needs of our brothers and sisters around the world. We have more than 9,000 physicians who claim African descent. There are over tens of thousands of nurses who claim African descent. Lawyers, architects, builders, teachers, preachers, artists, entertainers by the tens of thousands, many of whom call Christ Lord and Savior.

Between 1990-1991, there were 517,000 black men enrolled in higher education. More than half of that was in historically black colleges and universities according to (Information Plus 1980, from Wylie Texas). We have more than enough help to give.

In a recent report in the Philadelphia Inquirer, it was noted that over 89,000 African Americans graduate from college every year. When do we say we have enough education to help our brother? If we claim to know Him, He admonishes us in Luke 6:46 for calling Him Lord and not doing the things which He says we should do. John 14:15 Jesus tells us that if we love Him, we will keep His commandments.

One of the problems in the black church is our perspective of "affirmative action." We don't mind affirmative action when it comes to our getting what we deserve from the government. However, when it comes to doing our fair share in missions, we feel the pie is too small to share.

According to Jim Sutherland of Reconciliation Ministries, the typical African American church budget would read something like this; as taken from a survey of over 100 black churches in the southern United States. Church ministry to itself; building and maintenance 65% Emergency fund 26%; Funds going outside of the church 5%; of this, 4.2% for denominational expenses; UNCF 0.4%; Classic home missions 0%; Global Missions 5%. The total budget was $120,000 with a membership of 100-200 members.

There is more money spent on the men's breakfasts and women's auxiliaries in the typical black church than is spent on the primary call of going into all of the world to win souls for the kingdom.

The AME church reported on its 8,000 congregations with 3.5 million members. As of 1993 the total overseas ministry income was 250 thousand dollars. This represents seven cents per member per year or approximately $31.25 per church per year.

The NBC USA in 1992 was giving 51 cents per church member per year and when the cost of inflation is added in as a factor, this represents a 22 percent decline over 41 years from 1951.

It is obvious that we as black people have put our money where our hearts are. The average amount spent on entertainment by black people as recorded by the US Department of Commerce is $772, yearly, per consumer. whereas we spend a total of 22 cents per year in missions as a people of Christ. Just where are our hearts and where are our treasures?

What are His commandments? Are we our brother's keeper? Who is my brother? Who is my neighbor, the rich young ruler asked Jesus in Luke 10:29. Just who am I supposed to help Lord? Of course Jesus responded to the man's rhetorical question by reminding him that anyone in need was his neighbor. The man really didn't want to know the answer.

History is important. I am proud of being the black man God has made me. I am proud of the history that God has given me of a people who have overcome against great odds. I am glad that

God has shown His providence and provision in delivering our people from the evils of slavery and segregation in this land.

But I don't take my pride in where I come from or where my forefathers were born. I take greater pride in where I am going and that my heavenly Father has made me reborn. If I look at history alone then I will miss the present glory in the cross and the present and eternal glory of heaven. I am my brother's keeper. It is for this cause I was born in this life. It is for this cause I was reborn, born again into a new life.

We are our brother's keeper. Our brother needs the whole body to save him. Not just the yellow part, nor just the red part, not just the white part or black part. Our brother needs the whole body to save him.

We are our brother's keeper. Indeed, if I am not my brother's keeper, I am his killer.

GET A JOB

"I've been getting robbed!" That was the woman's expression as we closed one of our mission conferences in a Philadelphia church. I had to agree. I felt pretty much the same way. She was expressing her disgust and anger at supporting denominational missions for so long and never getting any report from the field.

"Why, we meet all the time and go through the motions of missions and we never see any of the work that's supposed to be getting done. Dr. Johnson can you tell me why we never hear of the kind of work you are doing? Why do we keep giving money and only get bulletins and handouts of pastors who have raised such and such amount of money and yet we don't see any work! We been getting robbed!"

I felt her anger. I only wish I could give her an answer other than, 'Yes you probably are right, you have been getting robbed.'

Why are you working with that white mission board anyway? That is the question I frequently heard when we first signed on with World Gospel Mission. I really don't know why to tell you the truth. I just felt called to Kenya and it seemed no one was interested in getting us there but these white folks.

I was sent by a prominent Philadelphia pastor to our denomination's mission headquarters. The pastor called ahead and made the appointment for me.

It was an old building in Philadelphia. The building had all of the charm that all old buildings have in decaying neighborhoods of the inner city. The windows were dingy and the air was dank and musty. The decor had not seen a change since the mid 1960's. The sun was bright outside but stepping inside you felt as though a cloud had covered it.

The missions chairman was there and one other staff person. I don't remember how long we met, it has been several years now. I do remember the context of the meeting. I was given the Annual Report of the mission board. I learned of the works supported in various parts of Africa. I learned of the various churches and saw the pictures of the pastors from those churches which supported the work of the board. I saw how much each church gave from across the nation. I read of how the staff used the money for the various administrative expenses.

I perused the book for more information on salaries and pictures of all of the stateside support staff. I turned page after page and learned more and more about this mission board. I saw how the mission board had sponsored several pastors to make a trip to various nations in Africa for short-term mission trips for preaching and evangelization. The only thing I didn't see was missionaries. It was obvious that this board had no currently serving long-term missionaries. I could not understand this.

Maybe I missed it. Maybe they were there. I just didn't see them. I started at the front of the book again. Nope. They are not there. I later learned that it had been over ten years since the board had commissioned a missionary.

Then the missions chairman walked in and began his efforts to recruit me. He says, to paraphrase him 'Dr. Johnson we have a small cottage hospital in a country in Africa.' We need a doctor to go and manage it. We have not had a missionary there for several years and I am not sure of the condition of the hospital. If you will go to the hospital, I will give you a salary here in the US and will support you while there. We will buy you a car for the time you are there and provide you a house for your return. There is no need for you to continue to go around begging for support. We can give you all you need.'

I sat and listened to the drivel coming from this man. I was really insulted. Why did he think I wanted to do missionary work. Was I looking for profits? Was I looking for some fame? He was offering me a job. I wasn't looking for a job. If I wanted a job, I would stay here in America. I wasn't looking for a job, I was looking for an opportunity to serve in Jesus name. Had they given me this, I might be with that mission board today.

I consider how many people sit in mission meetings today and have no idea where their support goes. I have never considered myself begging people for money. I have always considered that the people who claim the name of Christ actually want to do something in His name to show they are His and He is theirs. I just consider myself and my family a vehicle for them to express their love of Christ to others. This is not begging to my mind. Christians need to give because they pray to and declare they serve a giving God.

If God doesn't see the results of His giving to us, He might declare like that woman; "I was robbed!" As the book of Malachi declares, it is not good to rob God (Malachi 3:8) God states quite clearly there we will be cursed if we rob Him.

I trust we will challenge our leadership in our churches. Many of our problems in our fellowships are due to the fact that we have taken money given for foreign missions to use to build a parking lot or buy flowers for the altar. We need to help our missionaries feel the call and not help them to get a job.

Two men trapped in their MERCEDES Benz cars

She was their first-born child. While I was in the US for the year of 1999, she was admitted to the University of Nairobi's teaching hospital in Nairobi, Kenyatta National Hospital. This young woman, had just begun her studies at the university. Her parents, are friends of ours. They worked in a church hospital about a five hours drive from Nairobi. He is a physician and she is a secretary. For the sake of this story we will call them Dr. and Mrs. Lamu. This child, their daughter was the first-born.

Most children in Kenya inherit the family fortunes of debt, disease and desperation. Our friends, Dr. and Mrs. Lamu, did not want this for their daughter. They had labored for many years, sacrificing much of their own comfort to get their daughter into the best schools. The only way out of abject poverty in nations such as Kenya is education.

They were ecstatic when she made it into the university and hence rightly concerned when she was admitted there several months later with acute abdominal pain. It was a Saturday afternoon on which she was admitted. The Lamu family could not make the trip immediately to Nairobi and so they called a physician friend at the university hospital to alert him of their daughter's condition. The friend agreed he would look in the case and manage it until the Lamus could arrive on Monday morning.

As the story is related to me, because it was a Saturday, nothing gets done. Not even in the university hospital could you expect the x-ray tech to get an emergency ultrasound or x-ray. So the Lamu daughter lies in bed moaning all day Saturday and Sunday as the nurses record her deteriorating vital signs, her life signs and medicate her for pain. Her abdomen remains bloated, however, she receives no emergency surgical management and dies Sunday evening.

Dr. and Mrs. Lamu arrive on Monday morning to find their physician friend and to inquire how the management of their daughter has proceeded here at the Mecca of health care, the university hospital. The doctor friend goes on to talk about the weather and a variety of topics until Dr. Lamu interrupts and asks the inevitable; "Is my daughter dead?"

It is not good to tell bad news in Kenya. Your friend can be standing on your foot, but he pretends he placed his foot under yours. You never want to be the bearer of bad news. I can only imagine the pain my friends felt once their friend admitted somehow things had not gone according to their expectations. It is always painful to bring such news.

I have been on staff at the university hospital for over one year now. I only wish I had been there to consult and manage their daughter.

However, I was dining in Philadelphia. It was a free dinner in a very exclusive restaurant. That's why I was there. It was free! It was in the wine cellar of this exclusive restaurant in Philadelphia. Food that made the palate sing. Best of all, it was free.

There were notable people there, dignitaries, doctors, lawyers and people of high pedigree. I sat at one table and discussed life as a missionary and listened as others described the challenges of life as the nouveau rich. BUPPIES is what they were, the black equivalent of YUPPIES (you know, Black and Upwardly mobile People).

These are black men and women who had made it up the corporate ladder and were ready to make their impact in life, leaving a rich legacy of power, wealth and good deeds behind them. Unfortunately, many of the people with whom I sat were stuck on one of the rungs of this ladder.

I listened as one of the physicians I sat with complained of how difficult it was to make ends meet. He went on to tell me how depressing life was for him. His first daughter was in college and his second child was getting ready to enroll. He could not meet the tuition this year for the first child and had no idea of how he was going to meet the expenses for the next.

He was working harder and harder and falling further and further behind. He expressed how horrible this year was for him. I felt bad. I had seen families in Kenya who were not able to feed themselves. I had seen children stunted in growth to half the size for their age because of being malnourished.

I had seen whole families die because of meningitis and malaria epidemics. I had visited some of the poorest communities in the world, where parents literally had to make decisions of whether sell the half the children for food for some of the children or keep all of the children and watch them die. Even with the desperation I have seen on these Kenyan parent's faces, this man's depression was more exasperating. I told him, I would pray for him.

The dinner was over. I don't know who paid, but the 35 or 40 guests said their farewell and got out of there quickly, lest someone might hand one of them the tab. We went to the parking lot. This poor fellow whom I sat next to continued to tell me of his financial woes. I got more depressed now. I tried to find a way to be rid of him, lest he should spoil my whole evening.

I searched my pockets for my parking ticket. If I get it to the valet before this guy, I can get out of this mournful conversation. The van which the mission had loaned me for the year was very nice. It was a Ford Windstar. It was excellent for long trips for fund raising. It could fit all of the display items for our table, the literature, video projector and our suitcases. If we packed well, we could even fit our kids in.

As I got ready to hand my ticket to the valet, my depressed friend pushed ahead of me and handed his ticket in first. I guess that is alright..., him being depressed and all. 'Mine is the blue '98 Mercedes' he said! Now, I'm upset. What right did this guy have getting in front of me? What made him think he was more important than me? Just because his car costs more than mine is no reason for him to push ahead of me. Now I lose all sympathy and am filled with self-righteous indignation and jealousy.

The valet promptly disappeared to go find the car. Then the strangest thing happened. My friend leaned over and said; 'Would you loan me a dollar so I can tip this valet, I don't have any change?'

My feeling of sympathy for this fellow only deepened. I gave him the dollar. What would you have done, disappoint the valet? I only assume he gave the dollar to the valet and didn't keep it for himself.

Carol Davis, writing in the Philadelphia New Observer, June 30, 1999 had some interesting insights. She submitted the article as President of the Coalition of Black Investors. The article entitled Driving to the Poorhouse states that '29 percent of African Americans say their number one expense after basic necessities is their car payment, followed by their children's education. So while Black consumers have reached parity with whites in possessions and planned purchase of cars, African Americans lag behind in savings and investing.' We are trapped in our cars.

On one visit home from Kenya in 1992, I was working part time at the VA hospital in Philadelphia. I would take the trolley to work. I would carry a bag lunch on the trolley. I would think to myself, 'Michael, here you are a board certified general surgeon, working for the past eight years as a surgeon and what do you have to show for it? You are carrying a bag lunch on your way to work as a walk in doctor at the VA hospital making less money per day than you made as a resident.'

I cringed to think of what my former surgical patients might say if I met them on this trolley. 'Must have hit on some hard times, eh doc?'

My surgeon friend was aware of my dilemma. He decided he would take me out to lunch. I don't know why, but he did. I had hoped it would be to encourage me or offer me some help in support or even to volunteer to come over for a short time. He was after all from Africa. He had come to the US to train after completing medical school. He had since then, married and had bought a house and was living quite comfortably in suburbia.

He picked me up at the VA hospital. I was amazed at his car. It was a beautiful Mercedes, about the size of the trolley on which I rode to work. He greeted me warmly. He was glad to see me. I got on the trolley, oops, I mean in the car and we went to lunch.

It was as exclusive a place as you could find in west Philadelphia and it was frequented by the well to do and those who thought they were. I went on to tell my colleague of how difficult it was to find help for the work I was doing in Kenya and how badly I needed someone like him to come help. He rebutted that he would be willing to go to Africa, but times were so hard for him. This new system of managed care has left him unprepared for the consequences of this downsizing in health care.

He told me that he now needs to work harder just to stay where he is. He had his house payments, his kid's tuition, his mother in law was sick and he was not getting the reimbursement he needed for his services (Now don't be silly. He wasn't charging his mother in law. It's his patients we're talking about).

Furthermore, if he were to return to Africa it would have to be to his home country and that was not possible because of all of the political and social mayhem there. So rather than do anything for his home country, he had best stay here and do nothing.

My mind starts to wander. I am sitting here listening to this man pour out his heart to me about how unfulfilled his life is. He is serious. He is depressed. He sees no way out of this dreadful situation. How can he keep the payments up on his house and the swimming pool filled with water? Something's gotta' give! I think on how much water is in that pool. It is more clean water than I have seen in the majority of villages in the Pokot regions of Kenya.

There is a story about a man who was in distress because he had locked himself and his family in the car and left the keys inside of the house and couldn't get out of the car. Well, this may sound silly. Why not just open the door, you might say? They are trapped. There is no way out except to open the door. You don't need to dial 911 for fire rescue. You just need to open the door.

My mind goes on to wonder of my many friends who are trapped inside of automobiles, boats, houses and a variety of things with no way of escape. If they were to die today many of their families would be saddled with debt and stuff.

I reflect on these events only to question, who owned what, or what owned who. Did these two colleagues of mine own their cars, or did their cars own them? As Paul admonishes, I will not be controlled by anything (1 Cor 6:12). I don't believe there is anything wrong with wealth. I praise God for what He has allowed these colleagues of mine to accumulate. I fear, however, that they are under the power of these things and not vice versa.

I had known the freedom of this world. I had known the freedom to do my own thing. This freedom was such bondage. I found myself in bondage to my own lusts and desires. As I wrestled with my own slovenliness, passions and selfishness, I found I had no control, no power to control them and I had become the slave. This tendency to become enslaved is an ever-present danger in my life.

Every time I come home to the US, I am tempted to stay. After a few weeks of working and buying a new pair of shoes or a nice new tie, I begin to want one of those and one of these, and a this and a that. I find myself thinking that I can't get along without just a few of the things that sound like this and look like that.

I look around and see everyone else's is a bit shinier than mine and has a new insignia on it. I am ashamed because my brand is old, the kind that everyone wore two or three years ago when I was last home. " Everyone has moved on to bigger and better things or didn't you know that Dr. Johnson?" The spirit of covetous and envy rises in my heart. I am jealous and begin to think God has cheated me.

"Why don't you just stay here and work", my friends chide me? I am mindful of their concerns. The uninsured and underinsured are indeed a problem here in America. Current estimates are that more than 35 million Americans have no health care insurance. But while we wrestle with the problems of providing health care for this 12 percent of our population, I look across the ocean and see that 90 percent of the people of Kenya have at best rudimentary health care of any sort.

It is not that they are uninsured in Kenya, it is that even if they could afford health care insurance, there is no one to provide it. There are by present estimates one physician for every 450 Americans. In Kenya where I serve there is one physician for every 10,000 Kenyans. Just like in the US, the majority of these physicians are located in the cities. So the rural population which is 80% of the people, rarely if ever get to see a doctor.

Only 500,000 of Kenya's 28 million people have access to quality health care in Kenya according to the Chairman of the Kenya Medical Practitioners and Dentist Board in an article from the Daily Nation of May 1999.

It is common for many Kenyans to be born and die without ever having their birth officially recorded. They are known only to their mother in many communities, if she survives the birth, and their Creator. The father may be many miles away, looking for work, or just many miles away. The aged, near dead and infirmed are frequently left in the bush or forest and eaten by wild animals.

In Nigeria, according to a recent New York Times article of February 1999, the maternal death rate has risen from 800 deaths in 100,000 pregnancies to 3,000 deaths per 100,000 pregnancies. This is to be compared with 9 deaths in 100,000 pregnancies in the US.

A report in Kenya's Daily Nation newspaper of April 26, 1999, states infant mortality has risen from 61 to 74 per thousand. The report further states that 48% of the health care for the nation is delivered by hospitals like those in which I have worked, staffed by volunteers and missionaries.

As my friends and colleagues admonish me to stay here in the US and serve, I am confounded and confused. Am I doing the right thing? Are there alternatives to this ministry in Africa? Should I stay at home? What are my colleagues who criticize my going to Africa doing about home if they have such a heart for ministry to work here?

I spoke with a friend of mine a fellow black American physician who in fact is doing work in rural America. Dr. Ron Myers has served as a Christian missionary right here in the US When I asked him how much help he got from the black colleagues who criticize me for going to Africa, he responded' "Little to none." I began to realize people were not even willing to give of their time here at home in Tchula Mississippi where Dr. Myers was serving. Tchula Mississippi is a third world culture in a first world nation. Its residents are predominantly of African descent.

The health care statistics rival that of any undeserved population in the world. Mississippi has the highest birth rate in the country. 25% of all births are in teenagers. Mortality statistics show a racial bias with 37 deaths per 1,000 in African Americans, nearly four times the rate for whites in the state. A child born in

Chile or Malaysia is more likely to celebrate his first birthday than a black child born in the Mississippi Delta

A report in one paper describes Tchula as "a battered town with 1,900 people too poor to support a doctor." Dr. Ron Myers defies these statistics. As an African American physician he recognized the mandate for service to the poor. For over the past ten years Dr. Myers has been the only physician for this community. As of April 1999, as I write this, no one has seen fit to join him yet.

Black doctors complain they have been relegated to serving only the poor people. We complain that we have the chronically ill and the those with AIDS and terminal illnesses in disproportionate parts of our patient population. We have the medically indigent...., 'those people' to care for. Why should we take care of 'those people?' Why don't you just stay here Michael and take care of 'those people?'

During my several visits to Philadelphia since our ten years of being in Kenya, I have yet to be invited to any forum of black Physicians, neither those from Africa, nor her sons or daughters of slave descent. None seems interested in learning about the work we are involved with for 'those people.'

Have I really lost my mind? Are things really that bad over there or am I just imagining it to be so? Furthermore as they remind me of my call here and tell me of the joy of the work here, why are they so miserable doing what they do?

My mind comes back to my friend. Lunch is being served. It is a good lunch. It's even better, because I'm not paying. Everyone seems to be enjoying their lunch and mine would be more tasteful except for the painful look on my friend's face. Why is my friend telling me of the burden of keeping up the payments on his Mercedes which he can't get his family out of?

After hearing of his economic woes, I think to myself, 'how can I help this man? How can I make his day better? How can

I encourage him? Maybe I can pay for his lunch!' Then I remember that is stupid! I gotta catch a trolley. I need the carfare
to get home.

WORSE THAN AN INFIDEL

We used to call it "selling wolf tickets." That is what it means
when your bark is worse than your bite. When you talk big game
and don't follow through on your promises or your commitments.
You act like you are going to fight but you don't. You are just selling wolf tickets. We black people are selling wolf tickets when it
comes to Africa. We talk a good game, but we are not the least bit
interested in doing the real hard stuff it takes to go over and make
a significant impact for the continent.

Now these are very broad generalizations. I know that. I
don't mean to demean or reject the notion that some of us are not
doing our best to make a difference in the 'motherland'. However,
for so many of us who do nothing for the motherland, my retort
is: 'I am glad I aint yo' momma!'

We are not taking care of our home like people of other eth-
nicities. The Indians, the Pakistanis, the Jews, the, the Serbians,
the Chinese...,everyone takes care of their homeland..., the
Vietnamese, the Russians, the Irish..., all take care of home. We
sell wolf tickets. We are worse than an infidel. The Bible says that
the man who does not take care of his home is worse than an infidel (1 Tim. 5:8)

Of course we have our problems here at home. But the
Mexicans who risk their lives to come to the US and work hard
for less than a good wage in less than healthy places, send their
meager earnings home to help their own. The people of other nations sacrifice to come here and work in lowly positions to send
the little they own to their home.

We have succumbed to the idea that our position is so bad we can never help anyone until we have helped ourselves. We are worse than an infidel. The Bible distinctly says that the man who does not meet the needs of his own house is worse than an infidel. I believe that we are all of the house of God. But we as black Americans obviously have a special affinity towards Africa. We have ignored the woes of Africa and I believe it is reflected in our own status here in America.

We suffer from many of the same ills as Africa today. We have the highest rate of AIDS infections in the US (50% of US HIV infections are in African Americans while we represent just 13% of the US population). Africa itself has less than 14% of the world's population, but in sub-Sahara Africa, there are almost 80% of the world's AIDS cases.

Life expectancy for every group of Americans continues to rise, while for African Americans it lags behind, especially for African American men.

Poverty rates in black Americans are as high as 20% population and this is mirrored again in Africa where more than 40 of the world's 60 poorest nations are located. Illiteracy in Africa is epidemic in most nations having a rate as high as 40%. Again in America, our illiteracy as a people is higher than others. This is true for many reasons, not the least of which is that only recently have the majority black population which is still in the southern states, been legally allowed to read in schools which had reading materials. As we recall, separate but equal was only separate, never equal.

I contend that many of the problems we suffer as black Americans will persist until we begin to reach out to our home like every other people group have done. God wants us to take care of home.

We don't mind identifying with Africa as long as it doesn't mean sacrificing our comfort. We sing songs about Africa and write poems about Africa and take on African names. We say we can't afford to go to Africa and help, but we buy all of the artifacts and articles to identify.

We buy African clothes and cloths. We use our Visa cards to the limit and then say we can't give to mission work in Jesus name. The song we sing is no longer "All to Jesus I surrender, but all to Visa I surrender.

As stated earlier, with over 89,000 black Americans graduate from schools of higher education every year, we obviously have the manpower to send somebody somewhere to do some good some time.

We black Americans look at Africa and news about Africa and pretend that things cannot be that bad. We say rhetorically; 'It is just the news media making things look bad. After all, we know it was the white man who made the AIDS virus and infected the African with it. We know that the African nations would prosper if the white man would just stop interfering in the politics.' We villanize the white man and hence we don't have to go over and see just how bad it is for ourselves. We are afraid that if we do go and it is bad, we will have to do something about it.

So instead, we buy souvenirs of a land we dare not visit and then complain about the price of a ticket. We buy African beads and jewelry. We buy paintings of a place we dream about and hope the dream doesn't come true and we find ourselves there. Let's get real! If we would sell some of that stuff, we could easily afford the price of a ticket!

REAL MISSIONARIES NEVER READ INSTRUCTIONS

I can hear them laughing at me now. "Okay Dad, how'd you mess it up this time?" My daughter Christina is known to chide me gracefully. I can appreciate it from her the best as she has a sweet heart for making sure she doesn't hurt my feelings too badly. "Dad, just what are you going to do with all of those extra parts and pieces?"

"Hmmm" I think, "What am I going to do with all of these extra parts and pieces?"

In walks the less sympathetic one, Emmanuel. "Dad, I'm gonna call mom!"

Now I know I am in trouble, so I beat him to it. "Kay! Would you come here and help me with this thing. I think they sent the wrong tool kit with it, or something."

Kay promptly drops the chores of the kitchen and comes to redeem what is left of my manly esteem, to help fix the bike. "Well, where are the instructions" she quips?

"Oh. I put them over there somewhere." She goes on to help me out of my dilemma and stop the kids from laughing at me.

The only reason we are still with WGM is that Kay has read all of the instructions. She has read all of the rules. She knows the handbook back and forth. I peruse it to get a general understanding. For instance, I do know you are supposed to be a Christian and our headquarters are in Marion, Indiana. The rest of the details I have left to her. When I get to heaven, I suspect Saint Peter will ask me "Does your wife know you're here?"

This may seem like blasphemy. Reading the instructions is not necessary to be a Christian. There is not a single portion of the Bible which mandates you must read it. Jesus only admonishes us that the work of God is to "believe on the one whom He hath sent."(John 6:29).

Jesus says that 'eternal life is to know the Father', that is it does not depend on reading the whole manual. For this reason there are many physically blind deaf and dumb people who are Christians.

There are many people of limited intellectual capacity, or retarded in brain growth and development who are Christians.

I have met many illiterate people who have never read any Bible and love Jesus as Lord. They believe on the one that was sent. They know the Father and hence, have eternal life.

Who would know better how to be the real missionary than The Real Missionary? Jesus the Son of God, the ultimate beginning and end of all things, made the ultimate journey to time, to the ultimate destination earth and beyond to hell, to achieve the ultimate end our salvation from our ultimate end, hell to give us a new ultimate destination, heaven.

One of Jesus' biggest problems was that he refused to follow the directions, or read the instructions. He was not supposed to be born of a peasant woman, in a barn according to the rule-books. He was not supposed to be a man of low estate and low esteem. Jesus was supposed avoid company with thieves, prostitutes and murders. He forgot not to touch the unclean and was certainly not supposed to upset the well-established rules of the establishment.

Jesus neglected to follow the instructions and he paid the price. He should have avoided Nazareth, knowing full well that nothing good could possibly come from Nazareth. He did not recognize that the cross was supposed to be a thing of shame and instead, he made it a thing of glory. Jesus took the pieces of a culture steeped in tradition and pride and decided that for the glory of God the Father, he would make it non-traditional and humble.

Jesus took the extra parts and pieces he found in a little boy's lunch and fed 5,000 people. If he had read the instructions, he would have gone into town and found a caterer to do this. He would have formed a committee and delegated this responsibility. But instead, he took the boy's lunch and when everyone was full, he had pieces and parts left over.

The apostle Paul used the broken parts and pieces of a ship which ran aground and was able to save the entire crew and passengers of the ship (Acts 27:44). He then gathered pieces of wood and made a warm fire to help comfort the passengers and provide for their relief from being wet and weary.

I have found that by not familiarizing myself with all of the instructions, we have been able to strike out on some new ventures in missions. By not allowing the rules to dictate our thoughts, it is possible to invent. What things were not, now are. What things could never be done are now being done. What things were impossible and out of reach are now in our midst.

God gave us the pieces of ministry at Tenwek. This wonderful hospital which had served the community for so long, so well was succumbing to the onslaught of more and new epidemics of Tuberculosis and AIDS. We could no longer meet these needs by reading the directions given us; we had to find new ways to meet these new challenges.

I do know that familiarizing ourselves with the rulebooks is important. We need to appreciate the foundations from which we operate. However, which of us would rather watch Monday night Rugby versus Monday Night Football?

Which of us would rather watch Cricket over Baseball? How many of us would rather continue to rub sticks together instead of a match and lighter fluid.

We refused to read all of the instructions and God has given us freedom to help start internship in mission hospitals, work on establishing a residency program for family physicians, begin a street children's ministry and make inroads to the highest halls of learning at the University of Nairobi and Moi University at Eldoret. These ministries were not in the rule book.

Reading the rulebooks and instructions is something I am glad that I can delegate to my wife. My kids laugh at me. I get into a lot of trouble. But it has never cost me a dream.

I can dream about these parts and pieces which are left over just as Paul did when the ship he was on went aground. He was forced to make it to shore on bits and pieces of a ship. So when the kids laugh at Dad, I can point with pride at how God has allowed me to use the extra screws to fix other things. I am not sure how long the bikes will hold out, however, those extra pieces and parts are in use today.

WHERE IS YOUR COW?

I read the book "The Ugly American" and found out, I am really ugly. The kind of ugly that assumes that every Kenyan everywhere is only interested in knowing how green the grass is and whether there is rain in our part of the country. I have found that to my surprise there is a great deal of intellect. You just have to know where to find it. You cannot assume you know it all.

Now to be true, most Kenyans do have a different perspective on life. Even the most educated and enlightened Kenyans I have met will ask me "Where is your cow?" This is because the cow is an important part of life to the average Kenyan, about as important as the car is to the average American. Most of us cannot imagine life without wheels. We spend our lives trying to get greater and more comfortable mobility. We compare and consider the fine points and finance points of new and old vehicles.

Well it is the same with cows in Kenya, only more so. The cow is a vital source of nutrition for the family. In a time when drought and famine hit on a regular basis, the cow is the one reliable source for protein, except in times of drought and famine. Then a cow is an animal to be pitied as there is no food, no water and you watch the family investment, wither, stumble, fall down in the dust and die. In these very desperate times, families and communities will sell their cattle for as little as 100 to 300 hundred Kenyan shillings or the equivalent of one to four American dollars. That is cheaper than a Big Mac!

We are ugly Americans in a situation such as this. We don't know why people are so tied to the land of their birth. We cannot

understand the relationships of clan and tribe. We don't understand the strong pulls of tradition and custom which make people
behave in a way which is harmful to themselves many times.

How do we teach a chaplain in a hospital to accept that spiri-
tualism, demons and ghosts are distinctly important entities when
it comes to healing and yet not embarrass him with our sense of
superiority because we have the latest technologic advances?

How do we tell men and women that circumcising their young
in traditional ways is often mutilating to the body and mind and
can spread diseases which are incurable and yet allow them the
dignity of retaining the importance of some of these traditions?

What is the value of living in the middle of the poorest and
least educated people and never mingling with those who make
the decisions which impact the whole country? Can I be so busy
making decisions for people such as this that I miss the opportunity to talk about more than just cows and grass?

We have in many instances built our finest institutions in the
hinterlands, because this is where the poor people are. But as time
has moved on, we now need to ask more questions than "Do you
have a cow?"

We need to find out if the people involved in the decisions
about health and development want us to remain where we are
or do they have more important things for us to manage. We will
find this out from the educated and educators and not from those
whose livelihood consists of knowing if I have a cow.

Because we often associate with the poor, we only see Kenya
from their point of view. We can be subjected to the opinion that
no one has a vision in this country. We begin to be leaders in the
nation because we think we must do so by default.

We have no opinion about the needs of the country except
that "We need another cow." Because we as Americans know that
a car is more important than a cow, we move to the technological

god we serve and build bigger and bigger and bigger things in the hinterlands. All the people wanted there were more cows.

We have built million dollar institutions because it is what we understand. The hospitals in which I have worked are literally multimillion-dollar institutions. Multiple millions of dollars have been invested in capital building and equipment.

At no expense to these institutions and hospital, hundreds of physicians, nurses, administrative, technical, educational and spiritual personnel visit yearly, from overseas as volunteer workers. The operating expenses are underwritten by overseas supporters. After more than 80 to 100 years, these institutions are more dependent upon support from overseas than ever.

Mission and church hospitals now rival most of those which are managed by the government and private enterprises. Yet, if the missionaries pulled out today, they would come close to collapse. Is this what we want? Have we made the community depend on us, or was it inevitable? The proverb; 'It is better to know where to go and not know how, than to know how to go and not know where' comes to mind.

We have taught generations of Kenyans how to go, but have not given them directions as to where to go. We have built these institutions and staffed them with Kenyans who can perform rudimentary tasks by rote, but planning for contingencies, such as ordering before the inventory reaches zero, is not within many of the traditional cultural bounds. This is part of being the ugly American. It was the same when white Americans would look at the Negro of the good old days.

Negroes like all of those of African descent are supposed to be playful, spiritual and rhythmic. We are not supposed to be intellectual. We often even scare ourselves when we start to think.

This is why we excel at those things which do not threaten the establishment. It is okay to be Reverend, but not to be Doctor. It is okay to be a blues singer.

I have felt this attitude towards black intellectuals in my own life. I applied to college against the advice of my high school counselors who told me that I should not pursue college and certainly not medical school because I was not smart enough to do so. Having gone to Lawrence University in Wisconsin a highly ranked undergraduate school and University of Michigan medical school an even higher ranked graduate school, I recognize that such hurdles in my mind were difficult to overcome. I still wrestle and beat the slave attitude from myself as Paul states he wrestles with his flesh which is corrupted (1 Cor: 9:27).

Ali Mazuri says Africa has no winter. In his book The Africans, Mazuri states one reason for the lack of planning in Africa is there is no winter. Since there is no winter, planting and harvest can be year round. This subverts any need for long range planning. Missionaries come to the hinterlands of Africa without the knowledge of the intellectuals whose origin is in those hinterlands and have made it in the city. We need their insight.

We teach people the mechanics of how, but don't teach them where. We manage the where. We do the long range planning of what specialists should come to the hospital, what the formulary of the pharmacy is and which schools we should open for further specialists training. We let the Kenyans manage counting the money, as long as a missionary oversees it. We let the Kenyans drive the cars, as long as we keep control of the mileage and direction. We let the Kenyans do the grunt work, while we do the thinking.

Kenyans have adopted many of our traditions and customs because it is from a technologically advanced society. They don't see the moral corruption behind it. You can hear the most ghastly of American music and watch the most amoral movies and soap operas on any Kenyan television. American sponsored family planning in many instances mandate teachings on condoms to the exclusion of self-control.

It would be great if more Kenyan leaders took the advice of Ugandan President Museveni who was heard to say, 'We don't need foreign aid for abstinence.'

Distinguishing what is good and proper is not necessary because if it comes from the west, it must be the best. It is not unusual to see Monica Lewinsky's name on graffiti and the notion of sex without consequences is part of the popular literature.

We find Valentine's Day becoming just as prominent as Easter. Why give chocolates to a girl on a certain day, when her family is wrestling to find essential foods on every day?

In the struggle to become more American or western, we find Kenya adopting many of our holidays. We have shown them how to mimic our humor, but not where. We have given them holidays which mean nothing in the cultural context.

An extreme example of this is found in the April 1 1999 edition of the Kenyan newspaper, Daily Nation, which as an April Fools joke, announced the signing of a peace accord in Somalia. As war ravages Somalia, children brandishing weapons as directed by their 'war-lords', families starve and die from dehydration, typhoid and cholera. However, in an effort to embrace what is western, Kenyan newspapers make an April fools joke of the tragedy.

The retraction on April 2 read thus; About the "historic Somali peace accord" it was all in the spirit of April Fools Day. We apologize to any individual or party who may have been offended for that wasn't our intention. -

This is of course not a Christian media, however, it does point out the tendency of a nation like Kenya to embrace all that is western.

Martin Luther King preached that 'No man can ride your unless you don't stand up. When I ask my upcountry Kenyan friends and colleagues should missionaries leave the mission and church hospitals they resoundingly say; "NO! Never!" They are of the firm belief that they cannot manage such large institutions. They won't stand up.

"Why not?" is the question I shoot back at them. Their response is that; 'There are no honest, intelligent Kenyans of integrity.' They have become their own worse nightmare. They have come to believe the image that someone has had of them. They refuse to take the risk of standing up and being responsible for institutions that have been in their communities for over 50-100 years. Hence, if missionaries pull out of many of the hospitals today, most would scale back their services significantly if they would survive at all.

I often ask myself the same questions. Are there any honest Kenyans? Are there any Kenyans who will not take bribes for services which they are already paid? Can they be trusted?

As I look at government hospitals in Kenya I recognize it is hard to see how anyone could possibly call them hospitals. As you tour some of these institutions it becomes clear that the problems in management here is the same in other parts of the country. Many of the hospitals have no running water on the wards. Others have intermittent electricity and few if any ancillary services such as x-ray and laboratory. It is common to arrive at the hospital on a Friday afternoon with a ruptured appendix or obstructed labor and to die over the weekend because no doctor is available to manage your case.

Can't Kenyans do better? Why is there so much corruption? When you consider that every institution now in Kenya was formerly managed exclusively by the British or their underlings, (that is what they were), it is easy to understand the animosity towards government or any large, rich institution. Government and institutions never belonged to the people. They still do not. They belonged to the rich. Yes, they still do.

When the common man steals, he is stealing things that belong to the government and the rich. He is not stealing from himself or his family or his clan. It is this ambivalence towards the government and the general welfare it is supposed to protect which fuels corruption within Kenya. Everyone seems to be doing it, from the police to the statesman. Why not me?

Begging is an industry in Africa. It begins at the heads of state and extends to the lower ends of the most impoverished people. Whenever you walk the streets of Kenya, you are trailed and hounded by children, women, crippled in mind or body asking for something from you. The government encourages this not by edict, but by example. Kenya's government in the past would routinely wait for the announcement of foreign aid before setting its economic policies for each year. If there was little foreign aid, it was a sign that prices would increase. When there was little foreign aid, the donor countries were made to look like the devil in the press and other media because they have not given as they are expected to give. This attitude is reflected in the following article from the Kenya newspaper; The Daily Nation entitled; Africa's beggar states own billions overseas.

Begging bowl in hand, African leaders shuttle between their countries and foreign capitals in search of financial support, which often end up in overseas bank accounts. The capital held by Africans overseas is equivalent to 39 per cent of gross domestic product (GDP) compared with six per cent for Asia, according to the Ethiopia-based UN Economic Commission for Africa (ECA).

Analysts say if all the capital kept by Africans overseas was repatriated, the continent would move halfway towards meeting its external resource requirements.

Between 1982 and 1991, capital flight from the severely indebted, low-income countries in sub- Saharan Africa was about 22 billion US dollars, equivalent to about half the external resources required for steer development, according to the ECA. In relation to GDP, capital flight was estimated to be as high as 133 per cent for Nigeria, 102 per cent for Sudan and 58 percent for Kenya.

This constitutes a menace to, and flight diversion of resources from Africa's development. Nigeria is believed to have $50 billion alone outside the country, most of it, hot money, according to one UN official, himself a Nigerian.

Of the 18 countries the ECA carried a survey in 1991, Nigeria topped the list with a capital flight/debt ratio of 94.5 per cent, followed by Rwanda with 94.3 per cent and Kenya with 74.4 per cent and Sudan, 60.5 per cent.

A significant part of this amount, according to the ECA, originates from illicit diversion of public funds rather than from business incomes.

Africa finance and economic development ministers, who attended an ECA conference on: The Challenges of Financing Development in Africa, held in Addis Ababa on May 6-8, are also worried about brain drain. More than 30,000 Africans with PhDs now live outside the continent. An educated and skilled workforce is necessary to harness the technologies of the 21st century.

At the end of the conference, the ministers resolved to take the necessary steps to stem and reverse capital flight, including preventing macroeconomics policy lapses or policy inconsistencies, which are likely to trigger, or contribute to capital flight.

During the 1990s, one central African country president was believed to have had enough money to pay off his country's four billion dollar foreign debt. When asked, he declined. The reason: he was sure he would not get back his money. But for many years, he was in and out of Europe and the US begging.

"Capital flight is related to being in power and having access to domestic and foreign money and it is an issue that goes beyond the straight-jacket economics that is often used to explain its magnitude," noted a paper on capital flight by an ECA consultant.

The donor community is equally worried.

"There is increasing aid fatigue in my country and it is hard to convince my taxpayers to invest in Africa while Africans themselves don't seem to have confidence in their own economies. This is shown by the capital flight figures," Mr. Eveline Herfekens, Dutch Minister for Development Cooperation told the conference. The Netherlands is the single largest donor to almost every multilateral trust fund.

The ministers noted that without the cooperation of the developed countries, much of the continent's wealth remains stashed in Swiss and other European banks while the poor of Africa will continue to be subjected to austerity measures to meet external debt obligations to the same countries.

Again, to paraphrase, Ali Mazuri; he states that the African term is eating. Whenever an African leader comes into power, it is he alone who sits at the table full of food. Since the resources once belonged to powerful men overseas who ate up all of the food, it is now time for the new ruler to eat. He must eat it all.

No one else is allowed, except those chosen few in his cabinets and ministries of his own choosing. Eating in Africa is part of being in power and once in power, one must get fat.

This same attitude is reflected in black America when the riots occur in cities. 'It is not my property, so why should I car if it burns. The property represents the oppressor and they deserve to suffer.' Black Americans have never really been allowed to be accepted as citizens in America. When we finally begin to gain such respectability, we are reminded it is not truly ours as we don't experience equal protection under the laws. It was illegal for Blacks to celebrate the fourth of July in late 18th century Philadelphia.

America was not supposed to be our homeland, once all of the cotton was picked, the sugar cane harvested and the salt mines depleted.

We lack ownership of the nation and hence, you rarely see a yellow ribbon on a tree or a flag on every house in a black neighborhood. We fought in every war as segregated troops until the Korean War. In Europe during the World Wars, black American troops were often not worthy to be led by American officers and had to fight under the guidance of foreign leaders. When escorting prisoners of war in our own nation, those POW's would ride in separate cars so as not to be contaminated by black soldiers. We can identify with people who don't know ownership of the resources of their nation. We can be a valuable resource for ministry.

If we expect Kenyans to take ownership of the projects we initiate, we must recognize the culture of corruption as a natural outgrowth of a lack of identification and ownership of the projects. I believe black Americans can help fill this crucial need of helping people own their country.

The only way to change this is to incorporate Kenyans into the where as well as the how. Whom did we consult when we started these enterprises? Was it people who needed a second cow? Did we ever approach the intellectuals to ask what are the needs and how can we do this in concert? Was there anyone with whom we could consult? Is there anyone there now? Have we created a cycle of dependency similar to what is found in our own system? Are we rewarding nations for not becoming efficient? Are we sending messages through our mission agencies that we will tolerate corruption?

I know that as the Financial Comptroller of Tenwek Hospital, Kay had many occasions to sanction and penalize several hospital workers for embezzling. One case in particular involved the embezzlement of hundreds of thousands of shillings (tens of thousands of dollars) by three pastors of the church we work with. The case was taken to court and for at least three years, after many court dates, the hospital lost the case. It was ordered to reimburse the pastors for time lost on the job and to not seek any reparations for the money lost. No Kenyan was up in arms over the decision because, I believe, it was not their money. The missionaries could always underwrite the loss.

I think it is important for us to rethink how we can incorporate the intellectual community into the work that is before us. We now live in two cultures in the hinterlands of Kenya. There are missionaries who feel we must have a good car and the average Kenyan who feels they must have a good cow. The missionaries are always willing to buy the Kenyan a cow if the community will at least attempt to care for it. If there is no success at caring for the cow, well at least we tried and the Kenyan has a cow.

We need to involve a segment of the Kenyan population who understand that having a good car and a good cow is compatible. The intellectuals of Kenya must be consulted if we want to make Christ relevant to the nation. We work with the number 3 Pentium processor and expect people in the hinterlands to do so while many are not working with the number 2 lead pencil with ease.

We need to incorporate the intellectuals of Kenya into every decision making part of future ministries if we expect these ministries to flourish. Unless we do so, we will continue to alienate the governments and intellectuals in these societies and accomplish less and less as time goes on.

Kay and my efforts in this began when the Lord laid it on my heart to try to bring Kenyan interns to Tenwek Hospital. I had often wondered how I could get out from under the tremendous workload I had. Then I saw that all of us as guest physicians were suffering the same problem, no matter where we were.

Why not bring in Kenyan physicians to do this? This germ of an idea led me to make contacts with those people in Nairobi whose conversation went beyond; "Where is your cow?"

Beginning in 1992, I began to write and call the Ministry of Health officials in Nairobi. I met with them several times in the Nairobi offices and eventually convinced them that having the Kenyan interns rotate in mission hospitals could serve their interests and ours. There were a lot of details to work out, such as pay and housing, but eventually, Tenwek was assured of at least two interns from the University of Nairobi. This program soon involved other mission hospitals as well. Dr. Tim Fader of Kijabe Medical Center and I met with the Director of Medical Services and were able to start the internship program in 1995.

Tenwek has three Kenyan interns to date as do two other mission hospitals. Several of these interns have stayed on staff after completing their training which adds to the intellectual depth of staff and spreads the work load more evenly, relieving overworked missionary physicians.

Now Kay was extremely instrumental in these meetings. She was not just 'Dr. Johnson's wife'. My wife has a gift for knowing the heart of people and in her spirit of discernment, she would urge me to pursue these relationships with certain professionals and officials within the government and educational institutions.

Kay would also serve them the most wonderful meals you can imagine when they would happen by the hospital or region for any reason whatsoever. We took these professionals into our home and bedded them down whenever they came our way. This gift of ourselves was extremely instrumental in making a way for the future of health care in Kenya.

These efforts only succeeded because we were willing to dialogue about something other than cows. We had to recognize the intellectual community in Kenya as being real and desirous of being involved in the health care of the nation. To my surprise, I say to my shame, I met some of the most enlightened people of my life involved in health care in Nairobi. These relationships continued on until we were able to sponsor several Kenyan lecturers to come to Tenwek Hospital from the University of Nairobi.

It was indeed interesting watching the missionary doctors sit and learn from the Kenyan physicians visiting from Nairobi. It was unusual to have an American sit and listen to an African who was equal in achievement, learning and credentials. It was a challenge to the Kenyans who had to digest the fact that one of their own could possibly instruct the learned Americans, whom everyone knew was superior. Myths are very hard to destroy.

In 1994 I began to make inquiries about the possibility of Kenyan physicians who were in training within specialties coming to mission hospitals as part of their training. My hope again was that these doctors would see the mission hospitals up close and eventually want to stay and work in those hospitals upon completion of their training. The College of Family Medicine was an idea whose time had come. In point of fact, this had been a dream of many of the physicians of Tenwek and other hospitals. We were just too inundated with work to make the necessary calls and visits to get started.

I had the opportunity to attend a MAP program in Nairobi to discuss the possibility of beginning training programs within mission hospitals. I introduced this at Tenwek one day within a doctor's meeting and was laughed to scorn. I sweated through much derision and was told this was an impossible dream. We don't have the manpower, nor the resources. How could I possibly think that anyone could train Kenyans in mission hospitals?

However, because Kenyans and other Africans were willing to discuss the importance of training and were willing to be an active part of this training, we were able to persevere. Veteran missionary physicians had long envisioned such a program. Today the College of Family Medicine or COFAMED is quickly becoming a reality. When you allow people to tell you of their world view from their own world view, you can learn a lot.

We found that Kenyan physicians do things differently not because they didn't know to do them our way, but because they felt their way was better and they were willing and able to prove the logic and wisdom of their choice. We found they were right and we indeed could learn from them more than the nature and nurture of their cows.

I can now look back on these accomplishments with great feelings. I feel that God has allowed Kay and me to be a part of something that makes a difference for a lifetime for many Kenyans.

PEOPLE DO NEED BREAD

The Gospel is preached. The people are warmed by the words of this itinerant surgeon turned itinerant preacher. Just get saved, live right and everything will be alright. Somehow this message rings hollow to me. How do I live right? Well, personally, I stay with my wife and kids and earn a good living at the hospital. I provide for them the necessities of housing, food, clothing, education, health and even entertainment. This Christian life is easy! Just get saved.

Well obviously, there must be more to it than this. Don't people need something for life? What good is salvation if I can't feed my children. What good is salvation if I have to travel through matatu hell. What good is salvation if there is no educational opportunity for my children?

If getting saved is only for the next life, I do not want it. I need help on this side of heaven. As one member put it to his preacher Sam; "That idea of 'pie in the sky by and by is no good brother Sam if I need some ham where I am!'" Was Jesus being facetious when he said 'Man does not live by bread alone(Matthew 4:4)?' Was Jesus taking us for fools when he said the word of God was sufficient for life. (John 4:34) Was Jesus just kidding the disciples when he said, 'my meat is to do the will of Him who sent me'?

Oftentimes the church believes that when Jesus said "man shall not live by bread alone" Matthew 4:4, it meant the church need not address bread issues. Hence, the church has relegated these "bread" issues to ancillary services. The church meets to preach and teach about salvation from sin, but misses the opportunity to discuss freedom from famine.

Jesus did not make such a dichotomy of not ministering to the bread issues of life. In Mark 6:36 He makes it crystal clear that man does need bread. It would sure appear to be that Jesus was talking in circles. First he says man does not need bread, then he turns around and feeds five thousand people because he has compassion on them for their hunger.

Many Kenyans have learned to accept suffering because they have been told that man does not need bread. The old Marxist maxim of religion being the opiate for the poor comes to mind. Many Kenyans expect their houses to wash down stream and carry their drowning children along with the few precious belongings with them during the rainy seasons.

Losing a child to a flood is part of suffering. Losing a wife to prolonged labor and the oldest child to malaria is just part of life. Having a hand chopped off while working on a farm and loosing half of your blood volume before you can get to the nearest health care facility is what you expect.

Suffering is part of what you learn as you grow up in Kenya.

It is like learning table manners in America. The napkin goes in your lap. You say "Pass the butter please." You learn to hold the door open for a woman and close the door behind you.

In the same way, suffering is part of what a child learns in Kenya. No, there is no porridge today. You can't go to grade school because I don't have any money. I sold your sister for a bag of corn. It is just a different perspective on life.

I have watched women carry bundles and burdens equal to or greater than their weight for several kilometers. I have asked some Kenyan husbands; "Why does a woman carry things on her head when they could use a donkey or cart? Isn't it possible for these women to become more like women of the new Kenya?"

One husband answered; "These women are not of the new Kenya and never will be."

Carrying burdens is expected in Kenya. A woman is expected to search for water and wood every day. She is expected to work the field like any other beast of burden, despite the fact that there are plows and animals to pull the plows, the preferred beast of burden is the wife. She is expected to suffer.

Young men and women grow up in this culture learning to suppress pain. Boys are made to feel like little girls if they can't stand still in the cold morning air at age 13 and allow someone to excise their penile foreskin without wincing. Often the 'surgeon' is a drunken man who has not had a good night's sleep. I have seen the results of some of this handy work with amputated penises and other mutilations. Pain is part of growing up. You learn to persevere.

Many young girls still suffer the clitoridectomy or female circumcision, which involves the quick swipe of a knife as they are held down by the elder women. The results are less than predictable as the knife may not be sharp and could be rusty. Those young girls who don't bleed to death (some as young as 2-3 years old in some tribes of Africa) have just begun to suffer in this culture.

The knife has been used on others that night and the hepatitis passed from one girl to the next is later passed from child to child. The resulting scar at the vaginal entrance often makes these girls unable to have sexual intercourse and hence, once married, they are beaten and displaced by their husbands. This pain leaves both their bodies and psyches scarred. However they learn to persevere because it is part of growing up.

People have learned to persevere in Kenya. It is possible to perform a tubal ligation under local anesthesia in Kenya. The woman lies on the table and pretends to not be in pain as I put my hand in her belly. There is not enough sedation, but when I ask her can I give her something for pain, she grimaces and says 'no!' The Kenyan staff I am working with laugh at her as she begins to cry. "She is weak" they say! "She should be able to get through this without more pain medication." She is ridiculed because she hasn't learned to persevere.

Suffering is one art Kenyans have mastered well. The people of Kenyan accept that the schools will have no books and that the few dilapidated hospitals built by foreign money, will have no water in the water faucets, no drugs in the pharmacy and no electricity to run the broken down x-ray equipment.

In a May 1999 article in the Daily Nation, a Kenyan newspaper, the Permanent Secretary of Health had this to say of Kenyan's expectations of their hospitals; Kenyans think of our hospitals as places which will encourage them to die fast and not to survive. They think of hospitals as places which are dirty and manned by inefficient staff."

People are not surprised that famine strikes on a yearly basis. It relieves the parents of hearing a child cry for hunger or thirst or disease. They have accepted that God's mercy is to relieve the misery by relieving that child of life. Watching your family slowly starve and your livestock wither because of no water is a part of life.

Suffering is common to Kenyans. It is what is expected. The challenge is to distinguish this suffering from the suffering Christ talks about. When Jesus said 'man does not live by bread alone', he did not mean that man does not need bread. We must help our Kenyan brothers and sisters understand that the suffering they experience is not suffering for Christ. This is the suffering brought about by a system which robs them of their dignity and humanity.

Kenyans are able to take the old stale bread they have and make believe it tastes like sweet cake and luscious pies. They pretend the mold is just food coloring added for taste. They expect to suffer as part of life and I have actually had Kenyans laugh at me when I filter my water. A little cholera or typhoid is good for the system I guess. Dr. Martin Luther King in his "A knock at midnight" expounds that we must not let our brother continue to eat stale moldy bread.

In an effort to not become involved politically or socially, many churches are not encouraged to meet these issues. Many have ignored the injustices of the nation of Kenya because they do not want to be seen as politically involved.

Inadequate salaries, deficient public services and corruption in government are some of the bread issues on which the church does not speak. It can offend those who might have impact within their districts and the projects they cherish.

It is more expedient to allow the members of the community church to suffer from lack of bread, lack of health care, lack of education and lack of safe transportation than it is to teach people to address these issues in Christ's name.

I believe that if the Kenyan church and the missionaries were more involved with these bread issues and not the only, many of these development projects would be more sustainable. We have given the appearance that having the Bread of Life means people can do without bread for life.

The old bread of religion is not working. This bread tells us to become proud of our particular denomination. The old bread of tradition and tribe is not working. This bread tells us we are of greater importance or lesser importance than someone else. There is some precedence in the Bible for this attitude.

In Luke 10: 12-14, Jesus describes a man who was so impressed with his own service to God that he felt good enough to boast about it and remind God how he differed from the man who stood next to him, less worthy. Denominations have been divided in many places along tribal lines in Kenya and this has made the old bread of religion filler without nutrition.

The new bread of technology and science won't do either. These new breads are just old bread with a new topping of sugar. We are convinced that since it tastes different it is better. But science and technology from the west have not removed the problems of hate and despair from those societies. As we examine the good and bad of advanced communications and information, we see that the internet won't help what truly ails Kenya. Cable television has not relieved America of its spiritual hunger.

The next time you walk past a brick and mortar church building in Kenya and see an illiterate child, undernourished and thus small for his age and in ragged clothing, consider where'd we spend the bread? We must preach a gospel that provides bread.

The bread of self respect. We must help people find their all in Jesus Christ. We must help them be assured that they do not compare themselves to themselves (2 Cor. 10:12) and take pride in their heritage, but to take pride in who Christ has made them. They can thus be rid of tribalism and all of the evils that are part of that.

The bread of hope. Kenyans have given up hoping. They have seen programs and governments come and go and the economic, social and political situations are only getting worse. This bread will allow them to see that God is able through Jesus Christ to bring healing and wholeness to all of the situations of their lives. This bread will allow them to pursue new goals and new visions for their individual lives and the lives of their families and communities. No, man does not live by bread alone, but man does need bread.

LOAN GOD SOME MONEY/
BE A PART OF SOMETHING BIG

Proverbs 19:17 tell me that if I have pity on the poor, I am lending money to God. I liked the idea of loaning God money. I always thought He had enough already. Is it possible that I have more money than God? Do I really have to loan the Almighty some ready cash/ do I charge Him interest/ do I need to ask for collateral? What is this thing about loaning God money?

I look at this scripture in the light of mission work overseas with great delight. In point of fact, God has paid me great interest. Oh, he already put up the collateral, hung it on the cross. The interest he has paid has been the miracles he has given to me.

God sent me to Kenya to make me rich. He told me in Hebrews 11 that He would reward me as I diligently sought Him. He rewarded me with a family of which I can be. He paid me double interest with integrity and courage. He gave me the bonus of a reputation above reproach. When I returned from Kenya, I found that indeed, God had allowed the fields of medicine to be set afire and the money I thought I would be making had I stayed at home, was now much more difficult to secure.

I loaned God money when I became obedient in service to the poor. The scripture reads; 'have pity upon the poor.' But God knows, pity of itself is inadequate. Almost everyone feels bad when we see people suffering. Jesus did more than just feel pity, He actually did something about it. We are commanded to move on our pity and make a difference. I would advise you to loan God something. Give Him your life (Romans 12:1-2)

The most exciting thing about mission work is the great satisfaction that comes in seeing lives transformed by practical application of Biblical principals. I have had the joy of leading many patients to Christ. I have seen the faces of a husband and wife once separated by bitterness from adultery and the disease consequences, brought together with smiles as they find the strength to forgive.

I have witnessed Kenyan men whom I have had the chance to influence for Christ, go into kitchens, prepare and serve their wives tea. This is a miracle in Africa (and in much of America) as no man is supposed to serve his wife. I was able to convince these men of the importance of this act by referring to Jesus' desires for his bride the church. 'Husbands love your wives as Christ loved the church and gave his life for her' (Eph 5:25).

Loaning God money allows me to depend on him for the needed money for my children's education. Their college tuition is several times our combined yearly salary in missions and I had to remind God of this before we started. He reminded me that He never really forgot!

I have had the privilege of inspiring others to seek the Lord's will for their lives in missions abroad and at home. I know that God will use this book to further an understanding or at least cause enough controversy to bring about discussion. This is good payment for the loan I have given God.

Have you allowed your life to be squandered on small things? Are you working, sleeping, shopping, cleaning, sleeping and going back to work? I don't mean to belittle these important things in life. But wouldn't you like to be a part of something big? Wouldn't you like to get on God's big stage of life and make something happen for the future that will cause an effect to help millions of people? Be a part of something big. Get involved with God's plan for worldwide evangelization. Get involved with meeting the needs of people whom you will never know intimately, or personally. Start right there on Main Street and go to Outer Mongolia. God wants you to be a part of something big.

BE READY FOR SUDDEN DEATH/ LEAVE NOTHING UNDONE

"Fool, this night is your soul required of you." So reads the parable Jesus gives in Luke 12:20. Jesus further explains that our life does not consists of the things which we possess (Luke 12:14).

I can honestly state that if I were to die right now, I feel I have done all I have understood God wanted me to do to this date. I find great comfort in this. Oh yes I have made many, many, many mistakes. I have said and thought some ungodly, ugly things. Probably some of those things are right within this text. However, I know God's grace and mercy have allowed these all to be covered by the blood of Jesus Christ. I am not proud of these misdeeds and missteps, but neither do I bear the blame or guilt for them anymore. God has laid it all on His own son who died that I might be free from blame, guilt and judgment.

I have a friend who states jokingly; 'I want to die quiet and in my sleep..., like my grandfather..., and not in horror and shock...., like the passengers in the car he was driving!' Death can come suddenly. Are you prepared?

Those who walk with God have already reached the destination in life. John 6:28-29 records the question from the disciples as; 'What should we do that we may do the work of God?' Jesus replies; 'The work of God is to believe on the one whom he hath sent.' I do not return to Kenya to find what God wants me to do. I know what God wants me to do and that is to place all of my hope, dreams, desires and trusts in the name of Jesus Christ. I am not called to Kenya. I am called to Christ. I don't need to get on an airplane and cross the ocean to please God.

I have already arrived at the place where he wants me to be without ever moving from the place I presently sit. I am walking with God by believing in Christ. The disciples asked Jesus, "What can we do that we might do the work of God?" To which the master replied; "The work of God is to believe on the one whom he hath sent!" (John 6:28-29)

I believe that Jesus is the Christ, the Son of the living God and the only way to heaven. In doing so, I am already doing the will of God. In doing so, I will find myself doing things I would not normally do because I recognize my life is no longer mine. The evidence of my walking with God is my being willing to go to

Kenya. I will, as I stated earlier, lose my mind in His. I will allow him to do what he wants with my life as it now belongs to him.

As we return to Kenya in 1999 I have a great deal of apprehension. I look at the terror and disease and anarchy which are everywhere. I note the lack of clean water for the majority of people and famine in the land for millions. I know that as many as one in ten to one in three people I will operate on will have either hepatitis and or aids. I am fearful.

I fear for my wife and children who will travel over roads with armed and desperate bandits. I fear for leaving my children here in the US as they advance through college and, even though adults, still like to call home for advice and counsel.

The real issue is however, am I prepared to die? Have I done all I can for God? Have I prepared my family to carry on in my absence? Have we prepared our children to walk in the Lord even if we are not here to guide them? Am I ready to die?

This is my ultimate challenge to you as you read this book. I have meant to "comfort the disturbed and disturb the comfortable" as Bernice Albert King, Dr. Martin Luther King's daughter was heard to say. If you are disturbed about your own involvement in missions, mistakes and mishaps, rest assured, everyone who does service has made mistakes. If you are comfortable ignoring the issues, I trust this book has made you very disturbed.

Are you doing something so important for God right now in your life that if He called you home this moment, you would gladly go. Are you so successful in life that you are not enjoying it? Have you been removing cataracts from eyes or crushing bones and making crutches, healing the sick or making the blind man lame?

Have you put your life in order so as to be ready to die. You will die! Don't fear death. Fear a life that never risks anything to accomplish great things. Fear a life that is lived only to accumulate the wealth of this world and ignores what lies beyond. Fear a life which is lived filled with self concerns and self accomplishments, when we are all truly called to live for the good of others. Death would be nothing compared to a life that is lived for self. William Barclay states that "God will not absolve the man who is content to have too much while others have too little." A life without risk is a life without living.

Don't fear failure. Fear success at doing the wrong thing. A life without failure is a life without triumph. I used to enjoy beating my kids at chess and trivial pursuit…, it no longer was fun after awhile. I needed to fail. Failure is important to growth.

My greatest failures have not even been revealed in this book principally because I don't even know what they are. Only God truly knows where I have failed and where I have succeeded. Your perception of failure and success are not those that God perceives. Don't allow the fear of failure to stop you from doing great things for God.

I have no regrets in life except that I only wish I had done more in the will of God and less in my own will. If I had followed this line of reasoning throughout my life, I would have been a better father and husband. I could have been a better physician and surgeon earlier on if I had allowed Christ to have complete control when He commanded it.

I am convinced however, that God has never been impressed with my method as much as he is with my motive. We often impress others with our methods even though they never understand our motives. Jesus says we seek the praise of men, more than the praise of God. (John 12:43) It is a big problem in any work. I can think on the many marvelous things I have done in surgery and the many mistakes which I have made. God is not impressed with either. God is only impressed with why I did the procedure.

I will continue to be elated or emotionally wrung out over the successes or failures of my handling a specific case. God only looks at my heart and asks me why. It is because of this that I neither have to bear neither the guilt when things go wrong, nor claim the glory when things go right. I do need to study to do my best. I do need to strive to do my best. But I need most importantly to recognize that my best efforts are still meant to glorify God and not impress man or elevate myself.

I am often asked how many people did I lead to Christ. To tell you the truth, I really don't know. I haven't kept track of this. I do know I have been part of many people coming to know Christ. I've helped bring some to the Kingdom and helped send others on to glory. I just don't think it is important. There are so many variables to why someone comes to Christ and when they come to Him that it is truly impossible to number. So much seed was planted, so much water was poured and so many weeds were pulled before I arrived on the scene that I cannot begin to say who came to salvation since my arrival in missions.

I think the question about how many people I have led to Christ is as irrelevant as how many operations I have performed. I don't know. I do know that I for the 7 years I worked performed an average of 4-5 major cases per day. If you just count the weekdays and not the week ends, that adds up to a lot of surgery. I don't think it impresses God anymore than how many people I helped lead to him when it comes to numbers. He is more impressed with my motives than my methods, more aware of my notions about salvation than my numbers of years of service.

I know it is difficult to tell if someone is sincere about salvation when you stand over them with a knife in the operating room and ask them "Do you want to meet God?" This can be intimidating, especially when the man is wearing a mask!

"Well if it makes you feel better doc, I'll agree that Jesus is whoever you say he is."

Is this salvation? Do I count this man as a convert? I personally believe that if I asked him if he wanted to be a Hindu, he would have said yes. After all, I am the one holding the knife. I just try to not get into the counting game. I think that my God is not keeping that kind of score on me. He measures in ways I don't know about.

I do know this, I have had an influence. People have told me so and I believe it. Some of the influence was good and some was bad. The bad influences I have had were certainly not Holy Spirit led. I will probably never know of their full effect, else I become depressed. The good influences I will never fully know either, else I become too self impressed.

The writer of Proverbs noted this tendency in his own life when he stated; "Remove far from me vanity and lies: give me neither poverty nor riches; feed me with food convenient for me; lest I be full and deny thee, and say, Who is the Lord or lest I be poor and steal and take the name of my God in vain. (Proverbs 30:8) I don't want to take God's glory or take back the shame Christ has removed by his death on the cross.

With all of that taken into consideration, I still feel that I have no fault in what I fail, nor glory in my successes. Jesus has taken all of the fault and deserves all the glory. I am excited that I have to the best of my abilities lived my last several years actively pursuing His will under the guide of the Holy Spirit.

I have always wanted to be rich. I am a rich man. I read in Psalm 1 that God would do just that. He promised that everything I did would prosper if I would meditate on His word day and night. I look around me and see I am rich.

I have been given the opportunity and privilege of influencing the new millennium. I have been given arrows in my quiver in the form of four children who love the Lord and have a yearning to serve Him in their lives. I have been given a Godly wife who respects and honors me. I have been given a career which allows me to earn a good living and at the same time help people who are in desperation. I am a rich man.

I have been given a reputation of integrity and honesty, even when my heart and mind were filled with impure thoughts and desires. I have been given health and strength even when I often squandered these very things in my youth.

I have been given the joy of dreams. I have seen the dreams come true and God gives me new visions and new dreams and the means by which to achieve them. I am a rich man. I believe I am ready for sudden death.

My prayer is for all who read this book is that you yield your-self early to His control. There is no greater joy than to know you can stand on the last day of life and say..., I have done all that I could knowing what God had given me for this last day in life. Each day, any day could be your last.

ABOUT THE AUTHOR

1 Peter 2:9 But ye are a chosen generation,
a royal priesthood, an holy nation, a peculiar people;
that ye should show forth the praises of him who hath
called you out of darkness into his marvelous light:

The Johnsons were made to be a peculiar couple, called by a marvelous God. Dr.'s Michael and Kay Johnson have been involved in overseas missionary work since 1984. They were accepted to full time work with World Gospel Mission in 1989. Their ministry has taken them to several sites in Africa, including The Sudan, The Democratic Republic of the Congo (formerly Zaire), Ethiopia, Uganda; Tanzania and Kenya where they worked for 20 years, and short-term work in Haiti.

Their work in Kenya included working in mission hospitals (Tenwek, Kijabe and St. Mary's), where Michael functioned as surgeon, and Kay's responsibilities included administration and finance. God gave them the ministries of The Least of These, and A Prepared Place allowing them to work with a variety of indigenous Kenyan organizations. That work included providing food, clothing, and education and in-country adoption services for orphans. They were able to help build self-sustainable sources of food and water for rural populations. Their supporters helped fund the building of a full primary school and pay for secondary and college education for orphans.

The Johnsons returned to the United States in 2010, and currently serve with Miriam Medical Clinics to provide healthcare for the 'medically indigent' in Philadelphia and assistance for the incarcerated and their families. Gifts to Miriam Medical Clinic can be made online at **www.wgm.org/project/miriam**. Michael also serves as the medical director for the Hope Pregnancy Center in Philadelphia providing the resources to help families of the unborn make life affirming Christ honoring decisions.

Michael attended medical school at University of Michigan, in Ann Arbor, Michigan, and Kay is a graduate of Walden University MBA program in Minneapolis Minnesota. During their 44 years of marriage, God has blessed Michael and Kay with four (now adult) children and seven grandchildren. Their home church is the Tasker Street Missionary Baptist Church in Philadelphia.